CHINESE
FLOWER
ARRANGEMENT

SPRING ARRANGEMENTS

Colored woodblock print by Ting Liang-hsien, 17th century
(Moutan Peony, Iris, Narcissus, Camellia).

CHINESE FLOWER ARRANGEMENT

H. L. Li

DOVER PUBLICATIONS, INC.
Mineola, New York

Bibliographical Note

This Dover edition, published by Dover Publications, Inc., in 2002, is an unabridged republication of the work published by D. Van Nostrand Company, Inc., New York, 1959. The color frontispiece has been reproduced in black-and-white for this edition.

Library of Congress Cataloging-in-Publication Data

Li, Hui-Lin, 1911-
    Chinese flower arrangements / H.L. Li.
        p. cm.
    Originally published: Princeton N.J. : Van Nostrand, 1959.
    Includes bibliographical references (p.) and index.
    ISBN 0-486-42316-6 (pbk.)
    1. Flower arrangement, Chinese. I. Title.

SB450.7 .L56 2002
745.92'51—dc21

                                        2002067531

Manufactured in the United States of America
Dover Publications, Inc., 31 East 2nd Street, Mineola, N.Y. 11501

Contents

Illustrations

ILLUSTRATIONS

About Chinese Floral Arts and This Book

MUCH HAS BEEN WRITTEN in recent years on the art of flower arrangement as practiced in Japan, but very little on the floral art of China. Japanese flower arrangement had its origin in China, though through the centuries it has developed into a highly specialized branch of art by itself, quite distinct from its Chinese prototype. Its general principles, however, are still traceable to the basic canons of Chinese paintings, which are also the source of garden and floral arts in China.

There are distinct as well as subtle differences between the floral art of China and that of Japan. These are generally overlooked and there is a mistaken belief to many uninformed that the floral art in the Orient is the same in one country and the other. The floral art of China is in general less restrained and more colorful than that of Japan. The compositions are gay and life-like, while the serious and melancholy, as well as highly artificial arrangements practiced by some Japanese schools are not popular.

In China, floral arrangement is considered as an integral part of interior decoration, to be exhibited in harmony with one's everyday surroundings and not as an aloof and distinct cult. Although in floral art, as in painting and other forms of art, the Chinese have fallen into conventional patterns in more recent times, they, nevertheless, have not vested it deeply in formal rituals and rigid rules as the Japanese. In a way, the tendencies in the practice of these arts reflect the national characters of the two people.

There is also a certain randomness in the enjoyment of flowers and flower arrangements today. In China, on the other hand, much emphasis is placed on selectivity in the appreciation of flowers. Merits and virtues of the different flowers are carefully evaluated and the flowers graded according to relative standings. There are a few especially noble or charming ones that receive universal acclaim and become significant emblems. Others are noted for certain special qualities or for distinct beauty or for symbolism. Most flowers are enjoyed with definite sentiments and in complete harmony with the surroundings and background, all in keeping and enhance the artistic effect. Symbolism is of the greatest importance in Chinese flower arrangement. Another feature, and a special achievement, of Chinese flower arrangement is the distinct and discriminate selection of different flowers in association with different types of containers and accessories as well as other table decorations.

On purely aesthetic grounds, according to the Chinese tradition, besides the admiration of the beauty and elegance of a well-designed flower arrangement, emphasis is laid on the appreciation of the finer points of line and balance. A skillfully executed arrangement is equivalent to a composition in a painting, with the principles of design and balance carried out to perfection.

This work is an attempt to summarize the essentials of the art of floral decoration in China in the form of table culture and vase arrangement. The origins and underlying principles, as well as practical methods of preparing these according to the classical style, are given.

A very distinct contribution made by China toward the floral art is the highly developed craft of porcelain manufacturing. For centuries, the world looked toward China for the best pieces in flower vases. Chinese vases are now well represented in museums and private collections all over the world. It is possible for everyone interested in flower arrangements to study historical and modern Chinese wares in the leading museums in America and Europe. For this reason the account given here pertaining to the various types of classical flower vases in China is rendered in some detail with the hope that it may be of help to the interested flower arranger.

I

Influences Producing the Chinese Style

THE FLOWER AND GARDEN ARTS of China, like Chinese painting and music, like Chinese poetry and philosophy, are expressions of the artistic and literary genius of the people, an aspect of Chinese culture. According to the basic concept of Chinese philosophy, man is conceived as only one of the manifestations of nature and he is designed eventually to return to the cosmic element. This basic feeling of harmony with nature, furthered by the introduction of Buddhism from India in the first centuries after Christ, has become the dominant force in Chinese culture and history.

Because of the universal love of natural scenery and beautiful plants, ornamental gardening in China has largely developed along the line of idealization of natural scenery. Nature in the Orient is remembered in its entirety, the hills and streams as well as the trees and blossoms. Thus gardening becomes an effort to bring mountains and lakes to one's own courtyard by arranging rocks and trees and water to suggest an image of nature. In the quiet seclusion of these gardens, a man can repose in peace, contemplating the diverse moods of nature, and be inspired by its beauty and serenity. And by identifying himself with the cosmos, he can find new strength and happiness.

This naturalistic pattern of the Chinese garden has become the traditional style and remains to this day. Limitation of space imposed upon the average Chinese garden is apparently responsible in part for this trend.

1

Naturally, not every Chinese home could boast of a garden, yet the universal and intense appreciation of natural beauty has made it desirable that every home have some sort of planted area. Those who have limited means make their own small courtyard a miniature landscape. A few trees, artistically arranged with some shrubs and flowers, bring nature to the doorway of nearly every house. Thus developed the miniature courtyard gardens.

This tendency is carried further into the development of table plants or dish gardening and flower arrangement, designed primarily for interior decoration. It is a real and final effort to integrate nature with the daily life of every household desirous of having such an enjoyment.

The culture of table plants is collectively called in China "P'en-tsai," meaning pot or tray culture, or "P'en-ching," meaning tray landscape or scenes in vessels. Introduced into Japan, the former becomes "Bon-sai" in Japanese pronunciation, and the latter "Bon-kei," terms now better known to the western world than their Chinese prototypes.

Development of Floral Art

The exact origin of the art of tray gardening in China is not known. The art was evidently already quite advanced in the T'ang dynasty (618-906 A.D.). Tray gardens were frequently depicted in paintings of the Sung dynasty (960-1279). They appear even on porcelains of the sixteenth century preserved to this day, indicating their long and wide usage as decorations by that time. (Plate 3.)

Apparently flower art was well developed in the early T'ang dynasty, at the end of the seventh and especially during the eighth centuries.

During the T'ang period, China reached the most powerful and prosperous age in her history, and her boundaries were expanded greatly in all directions. The prosperity and grandeur of T'ang China attracted emissaries, traders, and travelers from such distant countries as Greece, Arabia, India and Persia. The culture spread to Japan, Korea, Annam and Tibet. In China, during the short-lived Sui dynasty (589-618 A.D.) preceding the T'ang, printing was invented. In the T'ang dynasty, the greatest accomplishments were achieved in literature. Also at this time, there occurred a

2

fundamental change in art, especially in painting, as flowers became more commonly represented, replacing animals and other motifs of mystic origins of the early arts. Garden art was also highly developed. Many new flowers, such as the celebrated Moutan Peony, were domesticated in the gardens for ornamental purposes.

The artistic Sung dynasty, which lasted for nearly three centuries from 960, was politically and militarily a weak one, but culturally one of the most splendid. It was a creative epoch in literature, philosophy and art. Garden art and floral art were both most highly developed. The use of flowers and plant materials for ornamentation and decoration, such as dish gardening and floral arrangement, also reached the highest level.

Construction of Dish Gardens

Dish gardens or miniature landscapes, developed at least thirteen centuries ago, are still very popular today. They are now generally made of stones and small plants placed in wide tray-like containers of bronze, porcelain or marble, varying in size from several inches to about two feet in length.

The construction of these tray gardens, from the oldest as depicted in ancient paintings, to the latest as appear in the market today, is very similar to that of a large garden. The main part is made up of curiously shaped rocks, suggesting in miniature jagged mountains and towering cliffs. A few plants or dwarfed trees or tufts of mosses grow out of the rock crevices, suggesting a forest. Miniature toys, such as little temples, houses, bridges, cottages, boats and figures, give life to the scene. The whole scenery is composed according to the principles and conventions of landscape gardening.

Pottery and Porcelain

The early development of floral art in China was apparently stimulated and aided in part by the artistic pottery and porcelain. It is but natural that ancient artists and craftsmen exploited fully the versatility and utility of these wares as vessels for growing and arranging plants and flowers. The relative inexpensiveness of ceramics in comparison with bronze, ivory and marble profoundly extended the popularity of floral decoration as an art among the general populace.

Although garden art was originated in China indigenously from

Influence of Buddhism

very early times, it was subsequently modified by foreign influence, notably the introduction of Buddhist culture. Buddhism, infiltrated into China from India, exercised at about the fourth and fifth centuries profound effect on Chinese garden and floral art, as well as on other aspects of culture. The great appreciation of nature was intensified by monastery architecture and gardening. New symbols and ideas in decorative art were gradually adopted. Flower arrangement received new inspiration and designs from the Buddhist passion for flowers and the carefully executed temple offerings. The artistic inclination and infinite patience and leisure of the priesthood contributed much toward the perfection of the art of dwarfing trees for miniature gardening.

Differences in China and Japan

Chinese horticulture and floral art were introduced into Japan around the sixth century and continued for several centuries thereafter. The effort of Buddhist missionaries was most significant. In Japan, floral art eventually developed into a quite distinct and much more stylized form than in China, heavily vested in rituals and conventions. Various schools have since appeared developing different techniques and using somewhat different materials. The different types of productions have also received distinct names and codes.

Floral art, though of much lesser importance than painting, the dominant art in the Orient, is primarily a form of pictorial art and follows the same general principles. In China, through the centuries, floral art has not become so restrained and formalized as in Japan. Its aim is to charm and to delight. There are no rigid codes and rules or ceremonial formalities. It, like Chinese painting, is primarily subjective, expressing the artist's own emotions as well as the intrinsic nature of the scene. It does not require rigorous observation of conventions as in some schools of Japanese arrangement.

Furthermore, floral decoration in China is not considered in itself an isolated object. It is but one of the details that merge into a complete scenery. For this reason, it is important that the arrangement of plants and flowers be made with due respect to their surroundings. Flower arrangement is closely associated with other table decorations, such as rocks, feathers, and all kinds of curios. It is also closely associated with furnishings, either flower tables to be used for it exclusively, or other furniture, such as tables and bookcases, that are often designed for combined use with floral decorations.

The widely varied architecture of the Japanese and Chinese houses accounts to a very great extent for the differences in the flower arrangements of the two countries. The Japanese house is generally a frame house. The rooms are small and are usually separated by sliding removable screen walls. They are covered with mats on the ground and are without chairs and other furniture except a few low tables. Floral arrangement is the main objective of decoration and the dominant feature of the living room. At the corner furthest from the entrance is a small alcove, on the rear wall of which hangs a picture scroll. In front of the scroll is a single vase with an appropriate flower arrangement. (Plate II.)

Effect of Architecture

As a result of the dominant importance and, consequently, the specialized development of flower arrangement in Japan, some of the influential schools have gone far into extreme and exaggerated curves so that the lines often appear too unnatural. In China, flower arrangement is generally more simple in nature and is more like that of the older schools in Japan, which were actually closer to their Chinese prototypes.

The architecture of the Chinese house is quite different from that of the Japanese. The Chinese house is built of brick on a wooden frame. Because of the customary large families, it is often of very large size, divided into many compounds, each with its own enclosed courtyard and sharing the one or more large reception halls. The rooms are permanently partitioned by walls. All rooms are furnished according to their nature. The interior decoration of the reception hall is more or less formalized, while that of the study and other rooms is not. The different rooms, with wide assortment of furniture and other decorations, offer innumerable possibilities for interior arrangement. *Floral ornamentations are made in complete harmony with the surroundings. They are never the only or dominant feature of decoration, but something to be integrated with the entire interior, thus forming an indispensable background of the household life.* These floral decorations for the interior include ordinary potted plants and lasting or temporary table gardens, as well as arrangements of flowers and plants in vases and other containers. (Plate I.)

Flower arrangement is thus closely associated and is to be made especially in harmony with furniture in interior decoration. A large vase invariably stands on the long table set against the inner wall of the main reception room. Table plants and vase flowers are often placed on large or small tables, combination book-curio cases, or flower stands. (Plates 4, 20, IV & V.)

Special Flower Stands

Flower stands are exceedingly variable in size and pattern. They may range from small ones to be placed on large tables to larger ones that stand on the ground by themselves. They are generally of "mahogany" color and with a highly polished surface like most other furniture. Though of endless variations, on the whole these stands emphasize the idea of simplicity of line, as is characteristic of Chinese furniture in general, and are strongly in conformity with the idea of contemporary furniture. There are also some special novel pieces for flower decoration. There is a type of detachable and divisible curio-and-flower-stand, or table, which offers a great diversity of arrangement. These have different patterns, such as triangular pieces which together form a square, rectangular or polygonal shaped table in infinite variations. There is also a round table consisting of two semi-circular tables. When combined, the table is big enough for playing cards or for serving tea. When separated into two pieces and placed against the wall, the pieces can be used for table plants or vase flowers.

Scenes with Plants "P'en- ching"

The culture of table plants undoubtedly had its precise origin in ordinary potted plants. In some cases the distinction between potted plants and table plants is not at all clear. However, in table culture, the chief aim is to present a naturalistic scenery in minia- ture, whether it consists of one or more plants, or whether it is decorated with stones or other objects. A single culture portrays a scene or scenery that is reminiscent of some famous mountain retreat, or suggestive of some general aspects of hills and forests

6

and lakes, the general idea of which being most appropriately conveyed by the name "P'en-ching" or tray landscaping. (Plate VIA.)

On the other hand, some table plants, especially those that are not of lasting nature, are not clearly distinguishable from flower arrangements. The use of cut flowers and twigs in vases, which is the most important version of flower arrangement, is clearly distinct. But the use of whole plants in trays and dishes is on the borderline between table culture and flower arrangement.

In general, table plants are more permanent plantings consisting of naturally small-sized plants or of larger plants dwarfed for the purpose. Frequent use of rocks is made, while flower arrangements include the use of all cut flowers and branches as well as the temporary use of plants of natural size. The distinction is not entirely necessary, as the two types can often be combined into one or used side by side, and the making of these cultures and arrangements follows exactly the principles of pictorial art.

The sources of our information on flower arrangement as practiced by the Chinese in the past can be derived from scattered references to the subject in the very voluminous literature on horticulture. There are also several outstanding books on flower arrangement. The most important is *P'ing Hua Pu,* or A Treatise of Vase Flowers, written by Chang Ch'ien-tê and published in 1595. It is the best work devoted exclusively to flower arrangement. It deals with vessels of all kinds, grading of flowers, technique of cutting and arranging branches, and methods for preserving flowers in vases. Another important work is called *P'ing Shih,* or History of Vases, by Yüan Hung-tao (known also as Yüan Chung-lang), who also lived at the end of the sixteenth century. He was a scholar and painter, and this work was also highly valued in Japan. It, also, deals with various kinds of vessels, grading and arranging flowers, and technique in watering and bathing flowers. It describes certain conditions that are compatible and incompatible to flowers, and circumstances in which flowers can be best enjoyed and appreciated. A third work entitled *P'ing Shih Yüeh Piao,* or Monthly Calendar of Vase Flowers, written by T'u Pêng-tsün in the early

Flower Arrangements in Old Books

seventeenth century, lists in tabular form the different kinds of flowers available for arrangement in the twelve months of the year.

Many treatises on plants and flowers for arrangement are also found in books dealing with the art of living. For instance, *Tsun Shêng Pa Chien,* or Eight Discourses on the Art of Living, written by Kao Lien-shêng in 1591, has interesting studies on vases, flowers, and flower arrangement. Another book called *Ch'ang Wu Chih,* or Records of Excellent Creations, written in the early seventeenth century by Wen Chêng-hêng, contains an excellent chapter on choice flowers and ornamental plants and their uses in making arrangements and table cultures. A more recent work is *Fu Shêng Liu Chih,* or Six Chapters of a Floating Life, by Shen Fu of the nineteenth century. In this now famous notebook, there is also a very interesting section on flower arrangement and related subjects.

A translation of Chang Ch'ien-tê's complete text is given in Appendix I. Excerpts from Yüan Hung-tao's work, as well as from other references mentioned above, are freely translated and quoted in the other chapters of this book.

In Paintings Prints Wood Cuts

Classical flower arrangement can also be studied from Chinese paintings and prints. The artistic Sung dynasty of the eleventh and twelfth centuries saw the greatest manifestation in painting as well as gardening and flower art. Flower paintings became very popular. From among the works of artists of the T'ang, Sung and later dynasties, many fine compositions of flower arrangement are now preserved in museums and private collections around the world. Flower arrangements are especially common as details in interior and courtyard scenes in painting. (Plates 2, 4 & 20.)

Closely related to paintings are woodcuts. Blocks for printing were used during the T'ang and Sung dynasties. In the Ming period, in the seventeenth century, multicolored woodcuts were developed. Some of the outstanding works were exquisitely done. The two most famous and beautiful of all these series of prints were the "Paintings of the Ten Bamboo Hall" and "Letter Papers of the Ten Bamboo Hall," first published in 1643 and prepared by Hu Cheng-yen, who based many of them on the designs of other

Plate I. CHINESE HOUSE
Above: Exterior of house and courtyard. (Courtesy of Mr. W. Allyn Rickett,
Philadelphia); *below:* Interior, a study (Philadelphia Museum of Art).

Plate II. JAPANESE HOUSE

Above: Exterior of house and courtyard. (Philadelphia Museum of Art); *below:*
Interior, a sitting room.

Plate III. TABLE PLANTS

Upper left: Buckthorn. A specimen trimmed and planted with the root system somewhat raised above the soil; *upper right:* Japanese Maple. A young plant trained and shaped by wire; *middle:* Juniper. A dwarf spreading form with branches trimmed to make a hanging specimen; *bottom:* Atlas Cedar. A young plant trained by wire to a leaning form.

Plate IV. A WOODEN FLOWER STAND
(Arthur J. Sussell, Philadelphia)

Plate V. BOOK AND CURIO SHELF
(Arthur J. Sussell, Philadelphia)

Plate VI. A TABLE LANDSCAPE

Upper left: Two Atlas Cedars trained by wire to produce wind-swept effect; stones and porcelain figures added to complete the landscape; *upper right:* Nandina. Arrangement of one leafy branch with two fruit clusters in a bowl; *lower left:* Pine. An arrangement of a single branch of pine; *lower right: Peony.* An arrangement of three red Peonies.

artists. Many compositions of flower arrangement were included, as well as prints of rocks, bamboos, fruits and birds. The latter is especially notable because in this work the technique of embossing was first employed, long before it was practiced in other countries.

A somewhat later series, of lesser quality but more renown, is the "Painting Patterns of the Mustard Seed Garden," compiled by Wang Kai and first printed in 1682 and 1701. This work was intended to serve as a beginner's manual of Chinese painting. There are instructions on painting various objects, including flower compositions, and on what the works of old masters looked like. The three works enjoyed tremendous popularity and were frequently reprinted in later years. These prints show designs in great simplicity. They illustrate classical interpretation of the subject and composition.

Besides these three major works, there are numerous other series of woodcuts of lesser extent, as well as individual sheets, many of them containing compositions showing flower arrangement. Most notable among these is a series of beautifully printed colored prints of flower and fruit arrangements by the artist Ting Liang-hsien. Because there is no Chinese illustrated manual of flower arrangement, we must turn to art objects such as paintings, prints, Coromandal lacquer screens, tapestries and porcelain wares to find classical Chinese arrangements.

COMPOSITION OF PLANT MATERIAL

The most essential thing is to have the proper design.

When twigs have the proper design, though they are tall and low and twining and twisting around, the major outline is still continuous.

When flowers have the proper design, though they are varied and pointing in all directions, each individual flower still looks delightful and does not become unnatural.

When leaves have the proper design, though they are sparse and dense and criss-crossing each other, they do not appear confused.

In the beauty and grace of plant material there are three major designs: pointing upward, hanging downward and inclining hori-zontally. But among these three, there are three further ways of arranging: branching, intersecting and recurving.

In branching, the design should show components high and low, and front and back, then it will not be ending all in forks.

In intersecting, the design should show components near and far and thick and slender, then it will not be all overlapping crosses.

In recurving, the design should show components upward and downward, horizontal and vertical, then it will not be coiled like the character "chih."

Then there are three more practical points, things to be empha-sized and avoided:

For upward pointing, emphasize gracefulness and avoid rigidity.

For downward hanging, emphasize an upward movement and avoid languishment.

For horizontal reclining, emphasize continuity and avoid flatness.

The Mustard Seed Garden.

10

II

Hsieh Ho's Six Canons

FLOWER ART IN CHINA, as already stated, is essentially a branch of pictorial art. Both in painting, as well as in flower arrangement, the artist, through his own gifts and projections, obtains first a vivid idea of the scenery and then proceeds to transmit his idea to the viewer. Flower arrangement, from very early times down to the very present, whether for temple offering or for home decoration, is composed in the same way as a picture or a print, following the same general principles. Actually, flower arrangement was often used as the subject of a scroll or a print, presented as a greeting to a friend. Flower composition was also often depicted as an accessory detail on large hanging scrolls.

The basic principles of painting, as accepted by all Chinese artists, are outlined in the famous Six Canons of Hsieh Ho. Hsieh Ho was a celebrated art critic and author, and an accomplished painter, who lived in the fifth century A.D. He formulated six principles as the essential components of a design, and these have influenced Chinese artists ever since.

The Six Canons

The first and most important is *rhythmic vitality*. There is a spiritual movement in the cosmos, running through every aspect of reality. It is essential that the artist have the desire to participate in the great life-flow of the universe. This is the prerequisite for all his work. For only by identifying himself with all nature will he be able to portray it adequately. Movement is the very life of Chinese pictorial art.

The second is *organic structure* or literally "bony structure." The fundamental structure of a composition should show solidity

11

of form. In Chinese painting, "bone" is a line which is continuous and strong from the beginning to the end. The "bony structure" is especially important in calligraphy, which is always considered in China as a major art form equal to painting. Its effect on painting is also very pronounced.

The third is *conformity with nature*. This means that the interpretation should be in accordance with the subject. Essential characteristics should be shown and superfluous detail avoided.

The fourth is *appropriate coloring*. The color should be applied in keeping with the true nature of the object. The color of the different parts should be harmonious with one another and with the surroundings.

The fifth is the *appropriate design* in the execution of the composition, and the correct placing of each object.

The final principle is concerned with *expression*. A composition should convey to the viewer the emotions and ideas of the composer. Composition by eminent masters are copied. Many ancient albums of classical compositions are studied to this day.

These six canons, though not literally followed at all times, become, nevertheless, the basic principles of Chinese art. These same principles are applied to floral art, not only in China but also in Japan. *The rules that are in force today among the various schools of flower arrangement in Japan are all derived from Hsieh Ho's Six Canons of nearly 1500 years ago.*

The composition of a painting in the classical Chinese style is often dominated by one major line together with several subordinate ones. The major line occupies the prominent position and is of the most conspicuous and dignified appearance, while the subordinate lines serve to enhance the beauty of the major line as well as to complete the design.

Application to Floral Art

The arrangement of flowers is done in a similar way. Each branch represents a line element of the composition. There should be a definite reason for the presence of each branch or flower stalk, as they should be used only to improve the quality of the composition or to suggest a definite idea. The whole objective is to have an arrangement whose composition shows rhythm and movement, the very life of Chinese pictorial art.

The following points summarize the essential principles in making flower arrangements in the classical Chinese style. They represent a more or less complete digest of authoritative works on the subject, together with interpretations of graphic representations of classical arrangement as appeared in paintings and prints.

Summary of Chinese Classical Style

(1) The arrangement of flowers in a vase should conform to the composition of a well executed picture.

(2) The arrangement should be appropriate for the season and for the occasion.

(3) There may be one or, at most, two or three kinds of flowers in a vase. In case one flower in different colors is used, the colors should be treated as if they were different kinds of flowers.

(4) The flowers should be arranged to appear alive and growing as in their natural manner. A neatly executed arrangement thus emphasizes irregularity, in a kind of studied disorderliness.

(5) Flowers should not be placed in pairs or in symmetrical patterns or in a straight row. It is desirable to have the twigs or branches in odd numbers.

(6) The elements should not be overcrowded, or too meager; they should approximate the natural conditions of growth of the plants.

(7) Slender and exquisite branches and flower stalks should be chosen, especially those of interesting shapes. The desired shape may be obtained by training during growth, or by manipulating the branches after cutting.

(8) In the same vase, it is desirable to have the flowers in one color, or in two or three harmonious colors. Strongly contrasting colors, such as white and red, should not be used together.

(9) When two or more kinds of flowers are placed in the same vase, these should be ones that naturally grow in the same environment or that suggest a single symbolic idea. They should be so arranged as to seem to grow out of one branch.

(10) There should be flower buds mixed with open flowers to break the monotony.

(11) The branches and flowers should be so arranged as to come out of the vase naturally as if growing directly from it. The mouth of the receptacle should be kept clear. Flowers and branches should not be too crowded, or too spread out from the mouth.

(12) When mounted in a wide-mouthed container or a basin-shaped vessel, the principal branch should be at one side and not shooting up from the center.

(13) The water surface in the container represents the earth from which the plants grow. Plant material below the water surface normally should not be visible.

(14) The branches or flowers should be in proper proportion to the size of the vase. Generally, if the vase is broad, they should be a few inches taller than the height of the vase itself. In the case of tall and slender or small vessels, the flowers should be a few inches shorter than the vase.

(15) In general the color or shade of the flower should contrast with that of the vase.

(16) Accessories accompanying flowers or plant materials should represent a definite idea and conform to the unity of the composition.

(17) When two or more vases are placed together, and when other table decorations are used at the same time, they should be of different heights and so placed as to give balance to one another, thus forming together the unity of a composition.

These various points summarize the main principles that were practiced in flower arrangement in the past and that are still being followed at present. They are not, of course, mandatory rules, but a carefully executed exhibition, which combines animation with classical restraint, always takes the more basic principles into consideration.

Historical Changes

Historically speaking, the style of Chinese paintings and arrangements in the T'ang and early Sung periods, about the tenth century and earlier, was more plastic, meticulous and detailed. Sometimes the contours were hard and, generally, bright colors were emphasized. From the tenth century on, the typical arrangement carried out to its perfection can be summarily stated as a compo-

14

sition with fine lines used sparingly and skillfully to suggest the most with the simplest means. (Plates VI, VIII & IX.)

In the art of the later Sung period, at about the twelfth and thirteenth centuries, when flower paintings were at their best, the emphasis was on the lyrical beauty and romantic spirit of nature. It is a type, as compared with the earlier ages, more generalized and impressionistic. During the Ming dynasty and in later times, from the fourteenth century until the twentieth century, the decorative element was even more strongly stressed, so flower pictures and arrangements were picturesque and ornamental, rather than symbolical. They were not considered as mere symbols of the cosmos itself, but valued for their beautiful designs and colors.

In the case of color, again the principles used in pictorial art are to be followed. Harmony is essential in the development of colors, and strongly contrasting colors must not be placed close together. When contrasting colors are used in one composition, it is desirable to have the light ones placed uppermost and merged gradually with the darker ones below.

Use and Meaning of Color

On the whole, in Chinese flower arrangements, *brightly colored and showy flowers are preferred.* Often these are set up against the dark green foliage of the same plant or some other plant. In many ways, *Chinese flower arrangements are more colorful and gay than Japanese arrangements.* (Plates VI, VII, VIII & IX.)

Colors have suggested meanings, and are so emphasized in floral arrangements and decorations. Red is universally considered as the color of good fortune, and is therefore used in weddings and other happy occasions. White, on the other hand, is the color of mourning, and white flowers are used as offerings at funerals. Yellow was formerly the royal color, and was also the color of temple decoration and architecture. Green is symbolic of eternal youth and everlasting quality, and thus all kinds of evergreens are used in decorating for celebrations.

THE ENJOYMENT OF FLOWERS

A great many verses on the enjoyment of flowers have been written by poets of all generations. The joyous see in them only happiness.

15

Here is a simple verse "On Cut Flowers" composed by Emperor Ming (557-561 A.D.) of the Northern Chou Dynasty:

Jade bowl receives flowers falling;
Flowers fall into bowl with scent.
Wine holds flowers floating above;
Flowers with wine come more fragrant.

Most poets, however, are more philosophical. As they enjoy the beauty of flowers, they also see in them the truth of life with a sorrowful tune. This comes from "On Flowering Trees" by the famous poet, Ch'en Ts'an, of the Tang Dynasty (618-906 A.D.).

Flowers of this year are as beautiful as last;
Men of last year are older today.
We, unlike flowers, can age, thus I learn;
Love the fallen flowers, my friend, and sweep not them away.

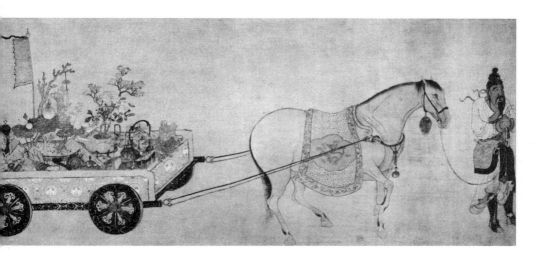

Plate 1. THE TRIBUTE BEARER

Detail from a painting on silk by an unknown artist, about 14th century. The
cart carries decorative materials for the court. Among these are vases with flower
arrangements and planted trays of Lotus, Magnolia and Rose. Flower arrangements and table plants were used long ago as gifts, presents and tributes.

Plate 2. FLOWERS AND TABLE DECORATIONS

A painting on silk attributed to the Emperor Huei-tsung (reign, 1101-1125),
Sung Dynasty. The large vase holds a classical arrangement of white Peonies;
three flowers are used, and one is in bud, a typical composition with three
elements of variable nature. Other decorations include a lamp, a piece of jade
on a low table and two rice puddings wrapped in bamboo leaves, these being a
special item for the Dragon Boat Festival.

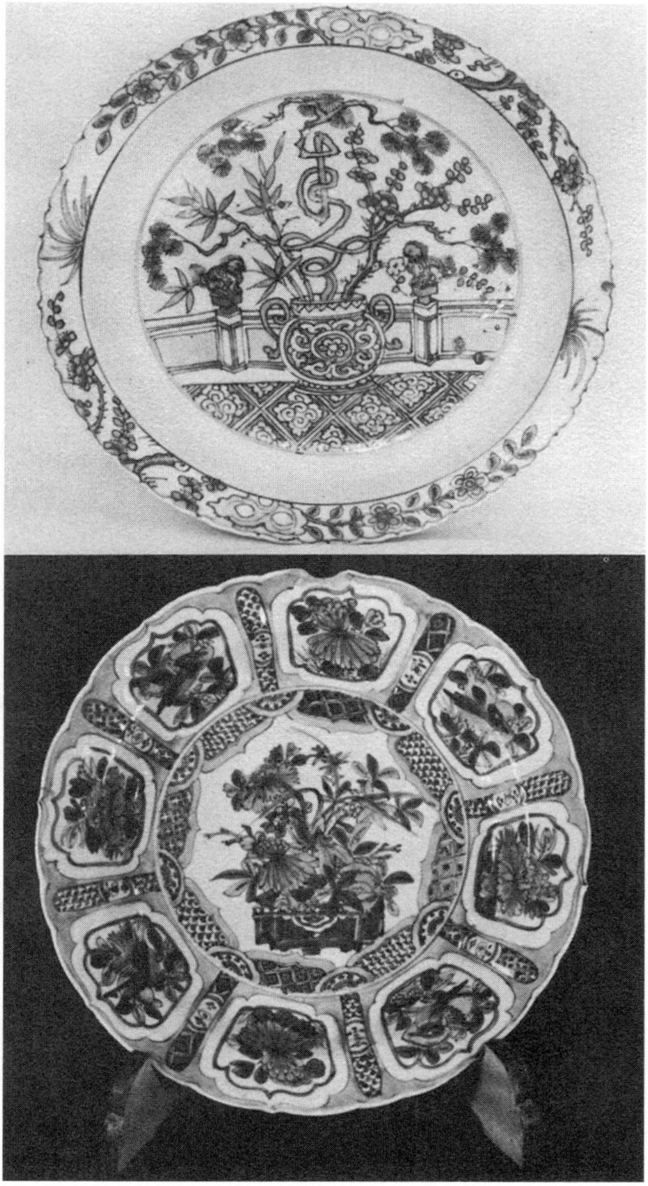

JOHN A. POPE.

Plate 3. PLANT ARRANGEMENTS ON
MING PORCELAINS

Porcelains in underglaze blue, 16th century, from the Ardebil Collection in Teheran. *Above:* Table culture of "The Three Friends of the Cold Season," Pine, Bamboo, Japanese Apricot. *Below:* An arrangement of foliage and Chrysanthemums in a basket, surrounded by a border of floral panels.

Plate 4. ARRANGEMENTS OF FLOWERS AND FRUITS

Silk tapestry, about 18th century. Arrangements of Peach Blossoms and fruits, Gardenia, Hollyhock and Orange in tall vase; Chrysanthemums in small vase; Rose, Ling-chih Fungus and Daisies in basket; fruits in bowl; and Hu-lu Gourd in foreground. Fancy stand at right is made for flower arrangements and curios.

III

Design and Composition

THE ESSENTIAL ELEMENTS OF COMPOSITION, in painting as in flower arrangement, are mass and line. In most paintings of the West, masses of color are emphasized in the compositions, while consideration of line is often secondary.

In Chinese painting and floral art, the composition is chiefly made of lines, with mass in a subordinate position. The main lines often appear as a few sweeping and powerful strokes. Stems, branches, flower stalks and flowers are the important elements. These are mostly represented by lines except in the case of larger flowers and foliage, such as those of the Peonies, where mass is indicated. The beauty of line is in general more emphasized. However, although in these larger flowers the style necessarily stresses aesthetic arrangement of color and masses, the charm of line is nevertheless not ignored. On the whole, flower arrangement in China is one of line and form as is typical for the essentially linear nature of Chinese art and calligraphy. The style, though less plastic than that prevalent in western art, is more so than the generally severe and austere one of Japan. *Importance of Line*

The placement of lines, together with the shape of the objects and spaces, suggests at the same time definite ideas and emotions. In a composition the major line or lines, therefore, conveys the dominant idea of the work, while subordinate lines add further ideas and give balance and unity to the whole composition.

These lines are not static, but should be forcefully and animatedly portrayed to convey a sense of movement and life. For instance, horizontal lines suggest peace and rest, while curved lines suggest *Horizontal Curve*

17

grace and motion. A most popular design is the horizontal curve, which is a horizontal line that moves upward at the ends. It represents the skyward direction of the rhythmic movement of man and nature in harmony. In the Chinese garden this is represented by the characteristic curved roof of the pavilion, and is one of the dominant features of the Chinese garden scene. In Chinese calligraphy, it is the circular swing of the downward side-stroke. In Chinese painting and flower arrangement, it is the conventional outline of branches of pines and the Japanese Apricot. It indicates strength overcoming difficulties, symbolic of endurance and perseverance.

Fig. 1. Typical line elements for arrangement.

Upward Lines of Pagoda and Bamboo

An upward directed branch suggests youth and aspiration, while a strictly upright one expresses dignity and strength. A direct skyward movement is represented by vertical arrangement. In architecture, this culminates in the pagoda. In pictorial art, it is represented by the contour of a tree. The monotony of a straight line is counterbalanced in the pagoda by the many tiers of gracefully downward-slanting roofs. Similarly, the upward movement of a tree is not represented by a simple straight line but is diversified by spreading branches and foliage. *A tree is thus pictured as a group of rhythmic lines bursting out of the ground. Branches should give a similar impression when arranged in a vessel.*

In the bamboo the stem is naturally of strict straightness. This becomes symbolic of straightforwardness. In pictorial and floral arrangements, the straight bamboo stem is displayed to artistic advantage through numerous distinct nodes, the clusters of branches, and the downward-slanting leaves. The straight upright stem, as counterbalanced by the downward-pointed leaves, is a good expression of the principle of *yin-yang* dualism. Bamboos are not depicted by a single culm, but always by several together to form a desirable composition.

Mass in Bouquets and Baskets

Bouquets and baskets of flowers, which emphasize masses rather than lines, are frequently uses as presents between friends. Bouquets are used for the celebration of hopes fulfilled, and of blessings of happiness received or anticipated. Baskets of flowers are indications of the love and good wishes of admiring friends. These decorations are used in weddings, birthday parties, and other celebrations. On these joyful occasions it is natural that emotions be less restrained, and consequently the arrangements are less sophisticated, sometimes even reaching the point of gaudiness. (Plates 18 & 19.)

Design as a Harmonious Unit

Thus, the various lines and, to a certain extent, masses of flowers and foliage, form the basis from which many designs may be derived. *A design is a harmonious unit. The different elements must agree with each other. The components must be in proportion and be balanced, but not in a symmetrical manner.* A good design will also show rhythm, the lines in combination giving the viewer a feeling of motion. (Plates VI & IX.)

Every flower arrangement, like any picture, can be reduced to a skeleton of structure. The simplest design consists of a single radical element or line accompanied by a few accessory ones. *The main element should be on one side of the center, and the accessory lines should show balance.* (Plates VI, VII, VIII & IX.)

Certain designs stem from some fundamental ideas in Chinese philosophy. The simplest, and a favorite, design is based on the principle of harmony of the *yin* (the female) and the *yang* (the male) elements, or the negative and positive forces of the universe, the cardinal principle of Chinese cosmology. It is the Confucian ideal of equilibrium and symmetry out of dualism, and subordination of the parts to the whole.

19

According to the Chinese idea, *yin* and *yang* are the forces that create the universe. Their perfect balance will establish cosmic harmony so that peace and prosperity can prevail. Their occasional conflicts produce thunder and lightning. *Yin* represents the earth, the moon, darkness, stillness and passiveness. *Yang* represents the heaven, the sun, light, motion and aggressiveness. In plants the upper surface of a leaf is *yang* and the lower *yin*. The upper or larger branches are *yang* and the lower or smaller, *yin*. Red is the most auspicious *yang* color, while green is that of *yin*. Each element represents one of the two phases of the same object, and thus the two should be in complete balance and harmony.

Fig. 2. Arrangements of two twigs can be either crossed or separate. The twigs are of similar shape and pointing in the same general direction, but one is somewhat longer than the other.

The *yin-yang* principle can be applied to flower arrangement in various ways. For instance, when two branches are used, one should be larger or longer than the other—the two should never be of the same size. Similarly, one branch may be placed above and the other below but not on the same level, or one may be ascending while the other is spreading but not in the same position. The two branches, although of different size or in different position, should nevertheless express unity and harmony. This can usually be achieved by having the two branches more or less similar in their general shapes, or by having them pointed in the same direction. (Figure 2.)

20

There is also the universal idea of the Trio of Geniuses, namely, *Heaven,* Heaven, Earth, and Man. It is a triangle with three levels, with *Earth and* Man placed between Heaven and Earth. The number four is indi- *Man* cated by the four seasons and by the points of the compass. The idea of Five Elements, namely, Metal, Wood, Water, Fire and Earth, is the ancient notion of the basic components of the cosmos. Five is a favorite design in China as it is the number of good luck and omen. The traditional Five Blessings are Longevity, Happiness, Peace, Virtue, and Wealth. Five is manifested in all forms of decorations. It represents the simplest and most expressive form of a group arranged in a complete circle. The number seven is another familiar design expressed in many forms.

It can be noted that odd numbers are favored in art designs and *Odd* are particularly emphasized in flower arrangement. It is easier to *Numbers* arrange an artistic design by using three or five branches of different sizes than by using four or six, which tend to fall into a symmetrical and thus less interesting pattern.

Several of these and various other ideas in the basic thinking and philosophy of the Chinese people are expressed in floral decorations and other pictorial arts. These same ideas were long adopted by the Japanese also, along with their other ancient borrowings from China, and they have also been emphatically and effectively expressed in the floral art.

As examples of classical designs, the arrangements of two or more *Placement* branches, such as those given in the painting manual of the Mus- *of Twigs* tard Seed Garden, can be mentioned. There are two arrangements for placing two twigs together. One, that of adding a smaller twig to a larger one, is called "carrying the old." Another, that of adding a larger twig to a smaller one, is called "leading the young." The manual states that "an old twig should be graceful and full of passion, while a young one should be delicate and full of charm. They should appear as two figures standing together, looking affectionately toward each other." (Plate VIII, Figure 3.)

For three twigs: "Although arranged in a row, they should not appear in equal heights, like a tied bundle of straw. They should lean away from each other on both sides, yet criss-crossing each other

21

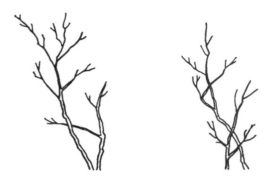

Fig. 3. Arrangements of two twigs of unequal size.
At the left, the small twig is added to the large one;
at the right, the large one is added to the small.

naturally." The proper arrangement of five twigs means a combination of three and two or four and one. This is a popular design much used in flower compositions. (Plates VID, VII, IX.)

With these ideas and designs serving as a basis, flower arrangements are made as aesthetic expressions or to convey some sentiment or emotion. Most frequently, arrangements are used to express con-

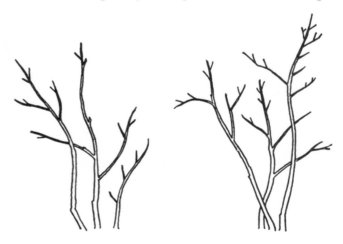

Fig. 4. Arrangements of three twigs.

22

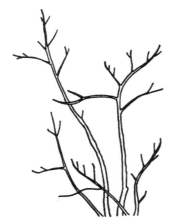

Fig. 5.   An arrangement of five twigs.

gratulations or various blessings, or to suggest some familiar tradition or precept.

There are many compositions made up of the symbolic meanings of the flowers. One of the most familiar and of the longest literary tradition is the "Four Princely Men," represented by the Japanese Apricot, the Cymbidium Orchid, the Bamboo, and the Chrysanthemum.

Symbolic Meanings

Fig. 6.   Twigs with three or five branches.

23

Several familiar compositions are designed for winter decoration and particularly for the New Year. The most widely known one is called the "Three Friends of the Cold Season," namely, the Pine, the Bamboo and the Japanese Apricot. A variation of this same theme has Pine replaced by Juniper, Bamboo by Nandina, and Japanese Apricot by Wintersweet. (Plate 3.)

For the New Year, a composition called Sui Chao T'u or "The picture of the levee on a New Year's Day" includes Narcissus, Nandina, Camellia, and the Ling-chih Fungus, all auspicious plants symbolizing good luck, longevity and prosperity.

Luck Symbols to Make a Rebus

The Chinese are particularly in favor of luck symbols and designate many flowers as emblems of luck, longevity and felicity. These plants are often used in combination as a pun phrase on an auspicious occasion. For wishing a friend long life on the occasion of his birthday, a frequent composition is made of four plants making a rebus, Ling Hsien Chu Shou, or "The blessings of longevity by immortals." It is composed of the Ling-chih Fungus, Narcissus, Nandina, and Peach. As variations, Nandina is sometimes substituted by Bamboo, and Peach by Pine or Podocarpus. A similar one, called T'ien Hsien Mei Shou, being a rebus for "Long life of a heavenly immortal," includes Nandina, Narcissus, Japanese Apricot, and Peach. The Magnolia, Crab-apple, and Peony, whose names collectively form a rebus of the popular expression Yü T'ang Fu Kuei, or "Wealth and honor in the halls of jade," is also of very common usage. (Plate 14.)

Lucky fruits make similar arrangements. The Apple, Peach, and a Pomegranate represent together a rebus, Fu Shou San To, or "Three abundances in luck and long life," the Apple signifying many blessings, the Peach many years of longevity, and the Pomegranate many sons.

Rocks Feathers and Insects

Besides flowers and other plant materials, accessories such as rocks and feathers may be introduced into a composition designed to express blessings or congratulations, or to convey some definite ideas.

In Chinese painting, a popular composition is made of flowers and insects. Butterflies, dragonflies, katydids, cicadas, and grass-

24

hoppers are among the most frequently depicted, many of them symbolizing luck or felicity. Shen Fu, in his Six Chapters of a Floating Life, describes an ingenious method used by his wife in making arrangements, namely, pinning different kinds of dried insects on the flowers to simulate classical paintings, to the great delight and admiration of their friends.

IV

Selective Association and Mechanics

As STATED BEFORE, flowers or plants selected for arrangements should conform to the season and occasion. When two or more flowers are used in a single arrangement, not only should they be normally of the same season, but they should also be compatible in color and texture and complement each other in their beauty and charm.

Selective Association with "Mistress" and "Maids" This idea of selective association is strongly emphasized in Chinese flower arrangements, and is often discussed at length in horticultural works. As an example, the *History of Vases* by Yüan Hung-tao can be quoted. This work gives a list of flowers that can be best placed together in the same vase. The author calls the most popular and beautiful flowers "mistresses" and selects for each a number of "maids" whose charm and beauty complement and enhance that of their superiors. (Plates 5 & 6.)

The list gives nine "mistresses," with from one to three "maids" each, as follows:

1. Japanese Apricot (*Prunus mume*)
    Winter Jasmine (*Jasminum nudiflorum*)
    Winter Daphne (*Daphne odora*)
    Camellia (*Camellia japonica*)
2. Crab-apple (*Malus spectabilis*)
    Siberian Crab-apple (*Malus baccata*)
    Chinese Crab-apple (*Malus prunifolia*)
    Early Lilac (*Syringa oblata*)
3. Moutan Peony (*Paeonia suffruticosa*)
    Rugosa Rose (*Rosa rugosa*)

26

Multiflora Rose (*Rosa multiflora*)
Banksia Rose (*Rosa banksiae*)
4. Herbaceous Peony (*Paeonia albiflora*)
Corn Poppy (*Papaver rhoeas*)
Hollyhock (*Althaea rosea*)
5. Pomegranate (*Punica granatum*)
Crape Myrtle (*Lagerstroemia indica*)
Double-flowered Shrubby Althea (*Hibiscus syriacus*)
6. Lotus (*Nelumbo nucifera*)
Asiatic Sweetleaf (*Symplocos prunifolia*)
Plantain Lily (*Hosta glauca*)
7. Osmanthus (*Osmanthus fragrans*)
Cotton Rose (*Hibiscus mutabilis*)
8. Chrysanthemum (*Chrysanthemum hortorum*)
Sasanqua Camellia (*Camellia sasanqua*)
Chinese Begonia (*Begonia evansiana*)
9. Wintersweet (*Chimonanthus praecox*)
Narcissus or Chinese Sacred Lily (*Narcissus tazetta* var.
orientalis)

When to Cut

Chang Ch'ien-tê in his *Treatise of Vase Flowers* gives notes regarding the methods and timing of cutting flowers for arrangement. He says that flowers should be cut in the early morning. This is indeed very true as plants are more vigorous and healthy in early morning when their water content is at its maximum. Later in the day the gradually diminishing water content results in a temporary wilting condition. While plants will restore their water content naturally and periodically during the night, branches cut from plants in a temporarily wilted condition will not be able to regain their water balance as easily as when they are intact.

Selecting Woody Branches

A twig used for arrangement should be chosen with discernment, and should have the features most suitable to illustrate the expression desired by the arranger himself and to give the impression of a naturalistic exhibition. The branch is to be carefully viewed from all sides, to obtain appropriate perspective and to examine the subject from all the views possible when the arrangement is completed.

As noted by Chang and other experts of flower arrangement, branches of woody plants are much easier to select than those of herbaceous ones. Woody stems usually assume more variable features to choose from than the herbaceous ones. Also, herbaceous stems are either unbranched or little branched, while woody stems usually bear sufficient number of branches to exhibit more or less complete compositions by themselves. In order to acquire sufficient knowledge to pick desirable herbaceous stems for arrangement, it is recommended by authorities on flower arrangement to study paintings of flowers. Rarely is a twig ideal in its original form to show all the desirable features. After carefully examining the twig in different views, it is often necessary to trim its parts, removing excessive side branches, superfluous flowers and buds, and undesirable leaves. The twigs should be in general slender and exquisite but not dense and thick. (Plates VIII & IX.)

Curving and Holding Twigs

Even after trimming, the twig still may not show the desired expression. The side branches may be too close together or too stiff. The leaves or branch-tips may be turning in the wrong directions. These may be modified or corrected by using a few simple manipulations. When a curve is desired the stem can be bent and held in position for a while. In some cases, heating over a flame will hold the bend. In other cases, especially in large woody branches, an incision or crack can be made. A small piece of stone is then inserted in the crack. By adjusting the size of the crack and that of the stone, the stem can be bent in all forms at will. On the other hand, a weak stem can be strengthened by inserting one or two pins. However, these pins should not be visible.

There are various ways of holding the twigs in position in the container. In narrow-mouthed vases, forked sticks cut from any tree or shrub are useful. In wide-mouthed vases and flat receptacles, copper sieves and holders of various shapes and sizes are used. These stands are also made of lead or iron. Some of the small and low vases have built-in covered tops with several spouts to hold the twigs in position.

Shen Fu, an author and painter, in his *Fu Shêng Liu Chi,* or Six

28

Chapters of a Floating Life, written at the beginning of the nineteenth century, describes a method of making a support for chrysanthemums in bowls or flat dishes, which may be applied to other flowers as well. A piece of copper is used on which a number of nails are glued upside down. This plate is then glued to the bottom of the vessel. The glue used is specially prepared by heating a mixture of resin, elm bark, flour, oil and straw ashes until it becomes sticky. The flowers are tied in groups by wire and stuck on the nails in the desired positions. After this, the vessel is filled with water and some sand is put on to conceal the copper support. The flowers thus appear to grow directly from the bottom of the vessel.

Precursor of the Needle-point

When two different kinds of flowers are used together, they should appear as if growing from the same branch. It is often best to tie them together by string or wire in the desired position before putting them in the vase.

The proper use of water is most important in order to maintain freshness of vase flowers. Not only should the water be changed every day, but sweet fresh water is recommended. Rain water or spring water is considered the best. In former times, connoisseurs often stored rain water in sealed earthen jugs for future use in brewing tea or for flower vases. Yüan Hung-tao recommended that a small piece of red hot coal be put in the water when stored, to keep it fresh for a very long time. He also enumerated the choice springs and wells in and around Peking that gave water suitable for use in flower vases, and pointed out others to be avoided.

Kind of Water

MY TEN FLOWER FRIENDS

Brier Rose	a graceful friend
Jasmine	an elegant friend
Daphne	a distinguished friend
Lotus	a clean friend
Osmanthus	a fairy friend
Crab-apple	a famed friend
Chrysanthemum	a fine friend

29

CHINESE FLOWER ARRANGEMENT

Peony   a gorgeous friend
Mei   a pure friend
Gardenia   a Buddhist friend

Ts'eng Tuan-pai (Sung Dynasty)

V

Symbolism in Flowers

NEARLY ALL FAMILIAR garden plants in China suggest some definite ideas. They are often spiritualized and seem to have an inner meaning. In making flower compositions for arrangement or painting, the beauty of the flowers is enriched by their popular symbols.

Each principal kind of flower has a fairy in Heaven attending to its welfare. In addition, the Chinese have personified the spirit of flowers and have given it the name of Hua Shên, or A Goddess of All Flowers, whose birthday comes on the twelfth day of the second month of the old lunar calendar. On that festive day, trees and shrubs are decorated with red papers.

From very early times, the Chinese people believed in immortals who, endowed with great wisdom and vested with magic, roamed at will the sky, the sea, and the earth. The earliest folklore about the mystic isles in distant oceans as the abode of these immortals apparently inspired rock gardens and miniature tray landscapes. In later times, through tradition, the story of the well-known Eight Immortals was gradually formulated. These Eight Immortals were very frequently used in art decorations symbolizing happiness and good fortune.

Of these Eight Immortals, four carried plant decorations as their emblems. Li T'ieh-kuai, with crutch and gourd, and dispensing beneficial medicine and magic, was the most beloved figure in the folklore. Lan Ts'ai-ho carried a basket filled with flowers or peaches, the fruit of immortality. Ho Hsien-ku, the only woman of the eight, carried a lotus flower or seed pod in her hand. Han Hsiang-tzu, a mystic figure with female appearance, had a flute or

Eight Immortals

31

fruit basket or both, and was regarded as the patron saint of gardeners. These figures appeared in paintings and as art motifs in all kinds of decorations. Their appearance in the daily scene of the people has greatly popularized floral decorations, even among the poorest and least educated.

Flowers and Birds

In Chinese art, flowers are frequently associated with insects and birds, particularly the latter. Flowers and birds often constitute together a specialized form of painting. Like flowers, there are a number of more popular birds which possess certain notable features and thus assume symbolic meanings. These selected birds are often associated with certain particular flowers bearing similar expressions.

Flowers as Symbols

A plant distinguished by some special characteristics may become the symbol of an abstract idea. Others, because of myths, folklore, tradition, some well-known historical events, or a popular verse or prose, may become symbols of a maxim, a moral attribute, or a personification.

Tree Peony

The Moutan Peony or Tree Peony, because of the bold beauty of the huge flowers, is considered the most aristocratic of all flowers, and is known as the "King of All Flowers." It is the symbol of wealth and rank, and is one of the main motifs in art. The Herbaceous Peony is called the "Prime Minister of All Flowers," as it is second in grandeur only to the Tree Peony. The lofty position of the peacock among birds is just like that of the peony among flowers. It has long been a symbol of splendor. Peacocks and Peonies are thus frequently associated in pictorial and decorative arts.

Lotus

The Lotus, emerging from muddy water but unstained and radiantly beautiful, becomes the symbol of purity and nobility. It is also the sacred flower of Buddhism, appearing at the seat of gods and goddesses, and held in the hands of many deities. For instance, Kuan-yin, the Lord of Mercy, was usually shown in earlier times holding a bottle of heavenly nectar and a Lotus flower, the symbol of his purity. It is the most common art motif in connection with religious decorations. In paintings and other art decorations, the Lotus is closely associated with the egret, a white water bird with long legs and bill. This is one of the most beloved birds in China, considered beneficial to the farmers. The Lotus and other aquatic plants are sometimes also associated with the Mandarin duck. This extremely beautiful bird has long enjoyed a distinguished place in Chinese art and folklore as the symbol of marital bliss. It is always depicted in pairs.

The Garden Chrysanthemum, as the only notable flower of late autumn, when few flowers are in bloom, is symbolic of a recluse. *Chrysan-themum* It suggests the idea of splendor and fragrance in a cool silent atmosphere, as in contrast with the colorful and joyful spring. Its lofty and isolated position also makes it an emblem of a noble personality. By tradition and folklore, the Chrysanthemum is the flower of long life. Thus the Chrysanthemum, under different conditions, may express various ideas, such as gentility, fellowship, nobility, or longevity. Chrysanthemums and other autumn flowers are often associated with the wild goose, a bird which always travels in flocks and traditionally symbolizes loyalty and the autumn season.

Similarly with many other plants, the same plant may suggest *Meanings* different ideas according to various literary allusions, and also *in Fruits* according to the arrangement and combination of materials. When Peach and Japanese Plum blossoms are placed together, by literary tradition they together suggest brotherliness and symbolize friendship.

By tradition and folklore, the Peach fruit has long been the emblem of longevity. The Peach flower, because of its delicate pink color, is symbolic of a charming young lady. The bright pink blossoms of Peach and the tender young leaves of Willow are common sights of the Chinese country, and together they are frequently pictured as representing the most typical scene of the joyful spring. (Plate 4.)

The very popular Mei Hua, or Japanese Apricot, because it *Japanese* blossoms at a time when cold and bleakness prevail, when even the *Apricot* branches are flecked with ice and snow, becomes an emblem of perseverance and purity. The Wintersweet, blossoming also in winter and resembling the Japanese Apricot in habit, is similarly

33

cherished and praised, and is sometimes used as a substitute for Mei in symbolism. (Plate 19.)

The Japanese Apricot flower has five petals, the auspicious lucky number. The five petals of this flower thus denote also the Five Blessings, a universal emblem of felicity. Because of this, the Japanese Apricot is often associated in art with the magpie, traditionally the symbol of happiness and good fortune.

Osman-thus

Also from very long tradition, the Osmanthus symbolizes good luck in official promotion and literary success. It is also the emblem of the mid-autumn Moon Festival.

Pine and Crane

The most revered and distinguished of all trees is the Pine tree. Because of its ruggedness and its evergreen foliage, it suggests nobility and venerability. It symbolizes the majesty of a wise old man. In gardens and in paintings, the Pine is particularly associated with the crane. The crane is the most venerated bird in China, supposed to have lived to a great age. It has long been considered a symbol of longevity in Chinese art and folklore. It was associated with the tales of the mystic isles of the immortals. Thus the Pine and the crane symbolize together the longevity, majesty, and great wisdom which went with age in Chinese thinking.

The Bamboo is one of the most popular plants in China. As the culm is hollow inside and straight outside, it symbolizes humility and fidelity. It will bend in the storm but never break; it thus suggests constancy and wisdom, the noble and scholarly character. As it becomes stronger when it grows older, it is also an emblem of healthy long life. (Plate 11.)

Bamboo and Willow

From the aesthetic point of view, the Bamboo, with its tall slender stalks and long narrow leaves, is enjoyed for its delicate appearance. It is a favorite plant with scholars and painters, and is intimately associated with the home. Its presence not only beautifies the surroundings but also gives inspiration to the soul. One former scholar declared passionately that he could not live for one day without bamboos. Another claimed that it would be better to eat without meat than to live without bamboo plants.

The Willows are common trees in China, growing everywhere in the plains, especially along water edges. It is a tree of sentimen-

34

tality, much beloved by scholars and poets. The swaying branches are suggestive of the slender body of a feminine dancer, hence the term "willow waist." The slender branches swinging and weaving elegantly in the breeze give the feeling of attachment and devotion. In former times, willow branches were picked from trees and presented to friends who were about to leave for distant lands to signify close friendship. Willow branches also have religious significance. Kuan-Yin, the Lord of Mercy, in later ages was transformed into the Goddess of Mercy and, instead of Lotus, she used willow branches in sprinkling the nectar of life upon the sick and dying to purify and revive them. The Willow is associated in art and literature with the oriole, a small bird of yellow hue, which has been a symbol of spring, music, and joy since very ancient times.

Cymbidium Orchids are not noted for their showiness but for their exquisite delicacy, and more particularly for their sweet and pleasant fragrance. The fragrance of these orchids is called the "scent of the kings." The Orchid typifies the idea of charm in seclusion, as these plants are found among the deepest valleys in the mountains. The Orchid also symbolizes a noble personality as well as friendship built upon sincerity. There is a well-known saying that true friendship is like the fragrance of orchids, as it pervades you with its charm and gracefulness. (Plates 10 & 20.)

Orchids and Narcissus

The Chinese Sacred Lily, or Narcissus, is symbolic of wishes of good fortune and prosperity. It is one of the most popular flowers of the New Year festival. As it requires only clear water and clean pebbles to bring the buds into flower, it also suggests purity and cleanliness. (Plate 11.)

The structure of a flower or fruit may become symbolic of certain ideas. The very numerous pinkish seeds of the Pomegranate fruit, which appear in cracks when the fruit becomes ripened, are symbolic of fecundity, long considered a virtue in the Chinese social system. The fiery red flower of the Pomegranate is symbolic of the summer season as it ushers in the torrid days of the year.

Symbolism in Plant Structure

Another case of symbolism derived from the specialized structure of a plant is the Lily. The Lily bulb signifies harmony and brotherliness, because of its very numerous overlapping scales. The citron Buddha's Hand is the symbol of happiness and blessings because of its resemblance to the fingers of Buddha. The Bottle Gourd, used since ancient times as a vessel for wine or food, is the emblem of abundance or good luck. The Ling-chih Fungus is the symbol of felicity and longevity. (Plates 20 & XI.)

Twin Flowers as Good Omen

The appearance of two flowers on the same stalk is considered a freak of good omen. The owner of two flowers of Lotus or Chrysanthemum on the same head will regard this symbol of felicity as worthy of a celebration with friends. In former times, the occurrence of two heads of rice, wheat, or millit on the same stalk was proclaimed by the emperor as an event of jubilation, as it was considered an auspicious omen, presaging a good harvest, a peaceful reign, and a prosperous country. (Plate 8.)

Flowers of the Seasons

Flowers are most appropriate in indicating seasons of the year. Nothing can be compared with flowers to show the ever-changing aspects of nature. The Chinese people, being agricultural and flower-loving, have long recognized the closeness of flowers with the calendar. Although there are many beautiful flowers for each season of the year, it is now universally recognized as typical that Spring Cymbidium stands for spring, Lotus for summer, Chrysanthemum for autumn, and Japanese Apricot for winter. These flowers, because of their beauty or fragrance or other virtues, are among the most esteemed and cherished. Long traditions through the centuries indicate these four flowers as the distinctive representatives of the four seasons of the year. They appear together as motifs in all forms of floral decorations, in paintings and other arts, and frequently also in literature and folklore. (Plates 5, 6, 7, 10, 11, 18 & 19.)

Of the Festivals

Some flowers or plants are associated with the great annual festivals. The first festival of the old Chinese lunar calendar was the New Year. This fell usually in early February and was close to the date marking the beginning of spring. The flowers and plants for use as decorations include Narcissus, Japanese Apricot, Bamboo, Camellia, Nandina, Gourd and Ling-chih Fungus. (Plate 15.)

During the Ch'ing Ming (Clear and Bright) Festival in late spring, homage is paid to ancestral graves, and this means a trip

36

to the joyful countryside. The tender branches of the Willow and the bright pink flowers of the Peach are the plants of this occasion.

The Tuan Yang or Dragon Boat Festival was celebrated on the fifth day of the fifth month, often close to the time of summer solstice. At this time it was believed that evil spirits were beginning to lurk about. Among the numerous symbols of this season were the Sweetflag and the Artemisia, which were thought of as capable of warding off noxious influence. The leaves of the Sweetflag, which are sword-like, were hung above the door, often together with Artemisia leaves. The Artemisia or Mugwort, *Artemisia vulgaris,* is a medicinal plant, and was frequently used as a charm. It is held in superstitious veneration in China and is noted for its exorcising powers in Europe as well.

The special symbol of Ch'ung Yang (Double Nine) Festival on the ninth day of the ninth month is the Chrysanthemum, the emblem of autumn as well as of longevity. In former times, the celebration of this occasion in the imperial court included displays of Chrysanthemums and the drinking of Chrysanthemum wine.

The arrival of autumn was celebrated in the court in ancient times, although in more recent times it is no longer marked as a great annual festival. Formerly the Catalpa tree was specially associated with this occasion, as it was believed that the fall of the leaves from this tree marked exactly the beginning of the autumn season.

The winter solstice in the eleventh month was also celebrated by a special ceremony in the imperial court in former times. Until recently, it was still one of the main festivals of the year among the general populace. The evergreen twig of the Juniper is the symbol of this occasion and is used extensively as decorations. The "Three Friends of the Cold Season," the Pine, the Bamboo, and the Japanese Apricot form together a special emblem of the winter season. (Plate 3.)

For every month of the year, there are also selected flowers typifying the changing garden flora. In most of the garden books in China, there appears a floral calendar, in which one choice flower is chosen as typical of each month. This kind of floral calendar is

Of the Months

37

also frequently mentioned in the folk songs of the different provinces. One of the oldest and best-known calendars is the one contained in the Book of Rites probably of the third or second century B.C., in which one flower or plant is mentioned for each month, along with other notable phenomena in nature.

Because of the fact that the vast territory of China displays a wide variety of climatic and soil conditions, varied versions of the floral calendar are given as representing the characteristic floral world of the different parts of the country throughout the year.

The old lunar calendar was discarded and the solar calendar officially adopted in 1912. However, the lunar calendar, which had been in use for thousands of years, was until very recently still closely observed by the Chinese people, who recognized the many holidays and festivities according to its dates. Generally speaking, *the months of the lunar calendar fall from one to two months later than the corresponding months of the solar calendar.*

Floral Calendars
The following table gives, by months of the lunar calendar, the leading representative flowers of the twelve months as generally recognized in the lower Yangtze valley in temperate eastern China.

I.	Japanese Apricot	*Prunus mume*
II.	Spring Cymbidium	*Cymbidium viresens*
III.	Peach Blossoms	*Prunus persica*
IV.	Apricot	*Prunus armeniaca*
V.	Moutan Peony	*Paeonia suffruticosa*
VI.	Lotus	*Nelumbo nucifera*
VII.	Cape Jasmine	*Gardenia jasminoides*
VIII.	Osmanthus	*Osmanthus fragrans*
IX.	Chrysanthemum	*Chrysanthemum hortorum*
X.	Cotton Rose	*Hibiscus mutabilis*
XI.	Sasanqua Camellia	*Camellia sasanqua*
XII.	Wintersweet	*Chimonanthus praecox*

Of historical interest is T'u Pên-tsün's *Monthly Calendar of Vase Flowers* of the early seventeenth century. This work gives a roster of vase flowers for each of the twelve months of the year.

38

Three grades of flowers are given for each month: the leading ones, which he called "rulers," followed by two other grades called "ministers" and "subordinates," respectively. The leading or "ruling" flowers are as follows:

I. Japanese Apricot; Double-flowered Camellia.
II. Crab-apple; Yulan Magnolia; Pink-flowered Peach.
III. Moutan Peony; Yunnan Camellia; Spring Cymbidium.
IV. Herbaceous Peony; Champac Michelia; Silk Tree.
V. Pomegranate; Day Lily; Oleander.
VI. Lotus; Plantain Lily; Arabian Jasmine.
VII. Crape Myrtle; Summer Cymbidium.
VIII. Red Osmanthus; Osmanthus; Cotton Rose.
IX. Chrysanthemum; Litsea.
X. White double-flowered Camellia; Sasanqua Camellia.
XI. Red-flowered Japanese Apricot.
XII. Wintersweet; Single-flowered Cymbidium.

FRAGRANCE IN FLOWERS AND PLANTS

The use of fragrant plant material is traditional in China. Not only flowers and fruits, but foliage and rootstocks are also enjoyed. *Eupatorium stoechadosmum* of the composite family, for instance, was one of the most cherished plants in ancient China, and was called Orchid Herb. A wild plant, it is sometimes cultivated for its attractive foliage. Its chief merit, however, lies in the pleasing fragrance which it emits when dried. It is used for adornment by women, for interior decoration and in cosmetics. Another well-known fragrant plant is *Agastache rugosa,* a wild herb of the mint family, used especially for its medicinal effects. The Sweet-flag is planted primarily for its delicate and ornamental foliage, but it is cherished also for its fragrant rootstocks. These fragrant plants are all used in Chinese flower arrangements:

Leaves

Agastache rugosa	Agastache
Artemisia vulgaris	Mugwort
Eupatorium stoechadosmum	Orchid Herb

Flowers

Chimonanthus praecox	Wintersweet
Cymbidium virescens	Spring Cymbidium
Daphne odora	Spring Daphne
Gardenia jasminoides	Cape Jasmine
Jasminum sambac	Arabian Jasmine
Michelia fuscata	Banana Shrub
Narcissus tazetta orientalis	Narcissus
Osmanthus fragrans	Osmanthus
Prunus mume	Japanese Apricot
Rosa banksiae	Banksia Rose
Rosa laevigata	Cherokee Rose
Rosa rugosa	Rugosa Rose
Syringa oblata	Early Lilac
Viburnum fragrans	Fragrant Viburnum

Fruits

Chaenomeles sinensis	Chinese Quince
Citrus medica	Citron
Citrus sarcodactylus	Buddha's Hand

Rootstock

Acorus calamus	Sweetflag

VI

Flowers and Plants for Arrangement

ALL KINDS OF FLOWERS and plant materials, including vegetables, weeds and lower plants, can be used in making desirable arrangements. In China, however, some plants and flowers, because of their special qualities, enjoy greater popularity than others. By tradition, a few of the most esteemed flowers are used more frequently than the rest, in paintings, in flower arrangements and in other decorations.

The important criteria for judging the relative merits of a flower are shape, color, texture, fragrance, variation, time of blooming, and supporting features such as branches and foliage. Cymbidium Orchids, for instance, are esteemed for their quaint and artistic shape of the flower, the delicately colored petals, the simple yet graceful foliage and, above all, for the subtle fragrance. Japanese Apricot is cherished for the symmetrical five-petalled flowers, the romantic manner of the branches, and also for the pleasing fragrance. It's time of flowering during the coldest season of the year undoubtedly accounts to a great degree for its extreme popularity. Similarly, the blooming of Chrysanthemum in autumn, Narcissus in winter, and other flowers out of season are all important factors of their relative importance in horticulture.

Criteria for Judging

The size of flowers is not necessarily an important asset, but in certain cases, such as the Peonies, the huge size distinguishes them as the most aristocratic. The eminent place occupied by the Peonies, however, does not depend on their size only, but also on their colorful petals, great variations, and ornamental foliage. The most popular flowers are nearly all those that yield to extensive varia-

Size

41

tions in cultivation, such as Cymbidium Orchids, Peonies, Chrysan-themum and Camellia.

Fragrance

Fragrance is one of the most valued characteristics in Chinese flowers. Nearly all the more popular flowers are of pleasing scent, varying from the intense and strong, like Daphne, Banana Shrub, and Jasmine, to the more delicate, like Japanese Apricot, Narcissus, Osmanthus and Wintersweet, and the very subtle and refined, like the Cymbidium Orchids.

Chang's Table

The grading of flowers, though subject to individual tastes, is in many cases determined by common consent and acclaim. Various such lists are given in horticultural works. The most important and complete one is given by Chang Ch'ien-tê in his classic *Treatise of Vase Flowers* written in the sixteenth century, as given in the appendix of this book. The most popular flowers or plants for arrangement are given in nine classes, according to the order of preference.

In the translation of the above, Trifoliate Orange may not be the right identification. The name Chi-chu, now generally applied to Trifoliate Orange, is suspected to refer to some other plant in former times, but its exact identity is not known. The flowers and fruits of the Water Chestnut were esteemed as ornamentals in former times but they are now scarcely treated as such. The other plants listed in Chang's table have all remained as popular orna-mental plants to this date.

Popular Garden Flowers

Nearly all the popular garden flowers of China are now widely grown in all temperate countries, especially in Europe and North America. The great majority of these can be cultivated in colder climates, while others are hardy in warmer regions only.

Besides these choice flowers and plants, there are many other kinds of flowers and plant materials used for decorations, such as foliage, berries and other fruits, weeds, and even a fungus. Arti-ficial flowers also are incorporated. Among the most popular flowers with many variations, a few of the best varieties in each species are generally more highly esteemed than others, and are more commonly planted and used in making arrangements. The following notes concern the more important flowers and also some special materials for making arrangements.

CYMBIDIUM ORCHIDS

For making arrangements, the single-flowered Spring Cymbidium, *Cymbidium virescens,* the choicest species of the genus, is used as a potted plant and in table culture, *but rarely in vase arrangement.* The artistic effect concerns the entire plant, the flowers as well as the foliage. The outline of the simple and graceful foliage is a necessity, when effectively posed in a suitable setting, to bring out the charm and attractiveness of the plant. In painting, this plant is frequently depicted in ink only, giving it a silhouette effect.

The Spring Cymbidium has been treasured as a choice ornament since very ancient times. The best varieties are those with purple pedicels and green petals, while those with green pedicels and green petals rank next, and those with purple pedicels and purple petals third. All the other varieties are considered inferior.

The other species of Cymbidium, such as the Summer Cymbidium, *Cymbidium ensifolium,* and *Cymbidium pumilum,* have long many-flowered stalks and are thus more suitable for making arrangements in vases. These flowers became popular at a later age than the Spring Cymbidium. The flowers are not so fragrant and are generally of a more yellowish tinge. These species are raised in pots and used as table plants. (Plates 10 & 20.)

Although the Chinese species of Cymbidium are also in cultivation in Europe and North America as greenhouse plants, they are relatively rare, and not so common as other species of the genus from southern Asia that have larger and more colorful flowers.

JAPANESE APRICOT (MEI)

The species *Prunus mume* is of Chinese origin and has been cultivated in China as Mei since time immemorial. It was first brought to the attention of western botanists from cultivated plants in Japan, hence the name "mume" and Japanese Apricot, mume being the Japanese pronunciation of the Chinese character Mei.

43

In non-botanical literature, it is generally referred to as the "Plum," although botanically it does not belong to the Plum group but instead to the Apricot group.

For Tables   The Japanese Apricot is not only the most beloved flower of the poets and painters but also one of the most popular flowers of the general populace. This flower is noted for its charming appearance as well as for its pleasing fragrance. As winter decorations, it is used as a pot plant, for topiary work, and as a dwarf tree, for table culture and for vase arrangement. There are many horticultural forms in cultivation, the most esteemed ones being those with green calyx and pink petals. (Plates 3, 7 & 11.)

For Vases   For use in vase arrangement, the Japanese Apricot is distinguished as one of the few flowers that are adaptable for both large and small as well as tall or low vases. The flowers are small enough for very small vessels, yet at the same time large branches can be used for tall vases, large bronze jars, and other kind of vessels. The branches are always in sufficient variable shapes, some erect and straight, some crooked and spreading, to be selected for use in variously shaped vessels from tall slender to low bowl-like ones.

There is a kind of tall vase called Mei P'ing, or Mei vase, for the exclusive use of holding branches of Japanese Apricot or Mei. The mouth is small and is designed for a single twig, hence this vase is also known as a one-twig vase. (Plates 17 & XIVA.)

Qualities of a Twig   Ch'ên Ch'i-ju, an author of the Ming dynasty in the sixteenth century, named four distinct desirable qualities in selecting a twig of the Japanese Apricot. In the first place, the branches should be sparse and not densely crowded. In the second place, they should show aged appearance. In the third place, the branches should be slender. And lastly, the flowers should be mostly only partially opened.

On the whole, the Japanese Apricot is unique among flowers in that the main ornamental features consist of, on the one hand, flowers which are delicate and charming in their appearance and, on the other, twigs which are valued for ruggedness and venerability. The arranger must have an insight into these distinctive features so that the arrangement executed will show vigor impregnated with sweetness, such as is peculiar to this flower. (Plates 7, 11 & 15.)

The Wintersweet, *Chimonanthus praecox* (*Meratia praecox*), a deciduous shrub, blooming also in the coldest season of the year, is used like the Japanese Apricot and is also much treasured. The flowers are a waxy, translucent yellow and have a more intense fragrance. The cultivated varieties with larger pure yellow flowers are preferred to the small-flowered varieties which are purple in the center. The most cherished variety has nearly erect petals so the flowers appear as partially open all the time. The Wintersweet is a more shrubby plant than the Japanese Apricot, so large branches with aged appearance are more difficult to secure. Also, the branches are often less picturesque because they are arranged oppositely and therefore more regularly. (Plate 19.) *Winter-sweet*

The Japanese Apricot is now frequently planted in the warmer temperate regions in Europe and North America for its showy fragrant flowers. It is not hardy to the northern climates and can only be grown as a greenhouse plant. The Wintersweet is a little hardier plant and is much grown in England and sometimes also in the warmer regions of the United States.

CHRYSANTHEMUM

The garden and florist Chrysanthemums are now among the choicest and most popular autumn flowers all over the world. Numerous horticultural forms of Chinese or Japanese origins are now in cultivation in western gardens, including many of the fancier kinds, which are especially prized in Chinese arrangements.

The Garden Chrysanthemum is the delight of flower arrangers. Not only is it the only notable flower at the season when the floral world is much depleted, but the endless variations in color and shape of the flowers offer innumerable choice and selection. Another great advantage is the ease and rapidity in which the stem can be trained at will. While planted in pots or in the ground, selected stems can be tied with strings to assume desired forms. By removing lateral buds and leaving only the terminal bud on the branch, larger and more fully developed flowers can be obtained.

Among the numerous varieties of the Garden Chrysanthemum, those with unusual colors and very fancy shapes are preferred for vase arrangements. Generally only a few flowers in a slender vase are desired, although in flat bowls the number can be much greater. It is also better to use only flowers of one kind and color to a vase, so that their individual charm and beauty are not distracted. The flowers should show various stages of development from buds to fully open ones to increase interest. Several vases of Chrysanthemums, each of a different color or form, can be placed together to form a composition by themselves.

When placed in a vase, the whole arrangement should appear natural. The flowers should be so arranged as to come up straight from the vase and not lean against the mouth. They should not be overcrowded or too spread out. (Plates 4, 6, 11 & 19.)

Sometimes potted plants of small-flowered forms are used to produce flowers in large numbers. These may be arranged on bamboo frames to assume various patterns or to simulate picturesque scenery from a cascade to a pine tree. During the Sung dynasty, practice like this to secure these topiary effects was common. The poet Fan Ch'eng-ta of the twelfth century, who wrote a monograph on the varieties of the Garden Chrysanthemum, stated that "Experienced gardeners in Soochow, at the time when the plant is only about a foot in height, plucked off the tip. Within a few days two branches come out and these tips are again picked off. Every pinching produces further branching until in the autumn one plant may often bear hundreds or thousands of flowers."

PEONIES

Peonies are the aristocrats of all flowers in China. There are two species in common cultivation. The Herbaceous Peony, *Paeonia albiflora*, has been in cultivation in China since time immemorial. Many varieties have since originated in the garden. As vase flowers, the Herbaceous Peony is most desirable not only because of the beauty of the flowers, but also because of their lasting quality and their ornamental foliage.

The Tree or Moutan Peony, *Paeonia suffruticosa*, has been

domesticated since the seventh century during the T'ang dynasty when it appeared first in the imperial garden. There are now endless numbers of horticultural varieties in cultivation. The Tree Peony is often used as a table plant and is among the choicest flowers for vase arrangement. Because of the huge size of the flowers, large vases are desired and the arrangements are more suitable for high and roomy halls. This suits admirably the Chinese house because Tree Peony symbolizes wealth and honor and the reception hall of every house is always the largest and loftiest room. The Herbaceous Peony with more slender herbaceous stalks and smaller flowers can be adapted for both large and medium-sized vases. (Plates 10, 14, 18 & VID.)

Both the Tree and Herbaceous Peonies are now widely cultivated in European and American gardens. The Tree Peony, being more difficult to grow, is less commonly planted, but the Herbaceous Peony has now become not only one of the most important cut flowers of the florists, but also one of the most popular garden flowers of the world.

LOTUS

The Oriental Lotus is sometimes planted in western gardens but as yet it is not common. Once established, it persists indefinitely. As an ornamental plant, in lakes as well as in small ponds, it is a strikingly handsome plant worthy of more extensive adoption. In North America, there is a native species with smaller, yellow flowers, the only other species of the same genus.

Both the flowers and fruiting stalks of the Lotus are used for arrangement in vases. The seeds appear atop a receptacle which is narrow at the bottom and flat and broad at the top. This distinct and picturesque pod is highly ornamental and a very desirable item for arrangement. (Plates 8 & 18.)

The peltate leaves of the Lotus, because of their large size, cannot be used in small vases. The flowers are therefore often used alone or with other plants, preferably aquatic ones. The flower stalks are very long, and although herbaceous, they are quite rigid. These stalks are erect and in nature scarcely straight, but often

47

exhibit various desirable forms for use in making arrangements.

Although the Lotus is of great religious significance with both Buddhism and Taoism, the flowers are generally used as popular ornamentals for their aesthetic value only. They are frequently grown in specially designed large bowls for courtyard or interior decorations. In making arrangements, only large vases are suitable because of the huge size of the flowers. The flowers are picked in buds as they shed their petals readily after blooming.

NARCISSUS

Narcissus, or the Chinese Sacred Lily, *Narcissus tazetta* var. *orientalis,* is more often used as a plant in a shallow dish rather than as cut flowers in a vase. There are specially made dishes or bowls for its culture, a practice of long tradition. The culture of the bulbs takes long and careful tending until they are offered on the market for the New Year Festival. These bulbs are carefully forced for the occasion by the florists. Only clean pebbles and clear water are needed to bring these bulbs into flowers.

The bulbs are of different sizes. Sometimes they are single while other times several bulbs are grown together in a group. There are varieties with double flowers. A form with coiled leaves and shortened crooked flower stalk is produced by deliberate mutilation of the bulb scales during its culture.

The preparation of suitable arrangements of Narcissus needs constant care for a few weeks. The length of the leaves and flower stalks can be regulated by the length of exposure to sunlight. The directions of growth of these can also be controlled by light. A desired arrangement can thus be achieved with some preconceived planning.

The Chinese Sacred Lily is now among one of the many kinds of Narcissus for indoor culture in winter in Europe and America. Other forms of the species, though of European origin, are very similar in appearance. For adoption to Chinese style of arrangements, the plants should not be straight but with a slightly curving outline. Also, the plants are not to be planted in the container

奇苍帶露移來玩開句
名園入錦圖 堯先氏書

Plate 5. SUMMER ARRANGEMENTS

A colored woodblock print by Ting Liang-hsien, 17th century, showing an arrangement of Pomegranate and Day-lily in a tall vase; an example of combining woody and herbaceous materials. Other decorations include a square incense burner with lion on lid, a water vessel, a gourd-shaped vessel, a partially unrolled scroll, a carved seal, and a Buddha's Hand Citron on a Lotus leaf.

籬邊高致欺霜
冷靜伴書齋到
畫屏　亮先題

Plate 6. AUTUMN ARRANGEMENTS

Colored woodblock print by Ting Liang-hsien, 17th century, showing Chrysanthemums and Begonias arranged in a tall vase. Other decorations include an
incense burner, books and a bowl of Buddha's Hand Citron in the foreground.
A wide-mouthed vase at back contains scrolls of paintings and a "coral-tree."

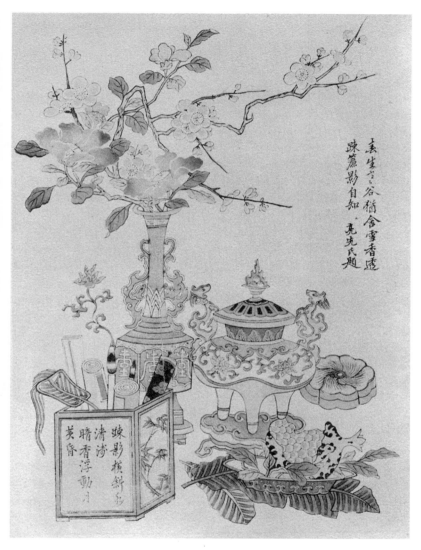

去生之谷橘舍雪香透
辣簾影自知・克先氏題

辣影横斜多
清淺
暗香浮動月
黃昏

Plate 7. WINTER ARRANGEMENTS

Colored woodblock print by Ting Liang-hsien, 17th century, showing an
arrangement of Japanese Apricot and Camellia in a tall vase. The Japanese
Apricot twig is of the typically twisted form generally preferred for this plant.
In the foreground, an incense burner, an ink stand, a bowl of Pomegranate fruits,
and a lacquer bin with scrolls of paintings.

Plate 8. PLANTS OF AUSPICIOUS OMENS

Painting by Lang Shih-ning (Giuseppe Castilione, 1688-1766, a Jesuit in the Chinese court), dated 1723. The auspicious plants and flowers in the vase are double Lotus blossoms and seed-pods, and double Millet Heads together with Arrowhead flowers. Doubled or paired blossoms or fruiting heads are considered of good omen.

en masse but singly or in small numbers, each with a desirable individual appearance. (Plate 11.)

OSMANTHUS

Osmanthus, *Osmanthus fragrans,* is an evergreen tree with dark green glossy leaves. It is not hardy to colder climates but can be grown as a house plant. In warmer temperate regions, it is now widely grown as a garden ornamental plant. The flowers are generally yellow and pleasingly fragrant. They are small and borne on short stalks clustered together in large numbers at the node. The choicest forms, considered best for arranging purposes, are the more floriferous ones with numerous flowers at the nodes forming dense globose clusters. (Plate 11.)

Osmanthus is a slow-growing tree and the branches are thus short and many-jointed, rendering them versatile for arrangements. Often it is necessary to remove excessive leaves to make the flowers more conspicuous. The golden yellow of the flowers is of sufficient contrast to the dark green of the leaves to present a pleasing combination.

MAGNOLIAS

The two species of Magnolias commonly cultivated in the Chinese garden are the white-flowered Yulan Magnolia, *Magnolia denudata,* and the purple-flowered Lily Magnolia, *Magnolia liliflora.* The relatively large flowers which appear conspicuously on bare branches before the leaves are very showy. A desired feature of these flowers in making arrangements is that nearly all flowers point upward. The generally shapely twigs, much branched and knotted at the joints, are very picturesque. The flowers, however, are appealing only in buds or when half-opened, as the petals drop off readily when in full bloom. (Plates 10 & 14.)

The Chinese species of Magnolia are now popular garden plants in all western countries. A hybrid of the two Chinese species, *Magnolia soulangeana,* originated in Europe in 1820, has purplish flowers and is now much more frequently planted than either of the parents. It is now one of the most popular flowering shrubs in both Europe and North America.

CRAB-APPLES

Several species of flowering Crab-apples are grown in China and these are now popular spring flowering shrubs in all western gardens. In the Chinese garden, these flowering Crab-apples are considered among the most beautiful of the spring flowering shrubs. The blushing pinkish flowers, of roundish shape, appeal to poets as well as to garden lovers. The beauty of the flowers is enhanced by the bright green foliage, which appears with the flowers, a feature which is not found in other popular spring flowering shrubs like the Japanese Apricot and the Peach.

Among the choice species are the Crab-apple, *Malus spectabilis,* and the Siberian Crap-apple, *Malus baccata.* As vase flowers, they are considered better than the other species because of abundance of the relatively small but showy flowers. (Plates 10, 13, 14 & 18.)

Another popular species in the garden is the Hall Crab-apple, *Malus halliana,* a species noted for the long pedicels of the flowers. While the hanging flowers are very attractive and appealing, they do not appear as ornamental in the vase as those having shorter pedicels.

ROSES

Roses were known in China from very ancient times and they first became favorite garden flowers in the T'ang dynasty. The best known Chinese species are the Rugosa Rose, *Rosa rugosa,* the Multiflora Rose, *Rosa multiflora,* the Chinese Rose, *Rosa chinensis,* the Banksia Rose, *Rosa banksiae,* and the Cherokee Rose, *Rosa laevigata.* The Chinese Rose, also called the Monthly Rose, is noted for the extremely long, nearly continuous flowering season. This species, as well as the Multiflora Rose and the Banksia Rose, have generally smaller and more numerous flowers. The Rugosa Rose and the Cherokee Rose not only have larger flowers, but are also more intensely fragrant.

50

All species of Roses are valuable for making arrangements. The large double-flowered forms like those of the Cherokee Rose are more appealing when they are in bud or only half opened. Sometimes these flowers can retain their best shape for a longer time if pins are inserted at the base of the petals while still in their half-opened state.

Roses are seldom used as bouquets in China, but usually in vase arrangements of from one to three or at most five branches, each chosen for individual charm in both the flower and foliage, or twig, and used alone or in combination with other flowers to present a harmonious design. (Plates 4, 20 & VIIB.)

The original species mentioned above, the Rugosa Rose, the Multiflora Rose, the Banksia Rose, and the Cherokee Rose, cultivated in China for centuries, are now also much planted in western gardens. These and other Chinese species played a very important part in the development of the modern garden roses which mostly have very complex parentage.

DAPHNES

The Spring Daphne, *Daphne odora*, is a choice garden flower. It is a relatively late arrival in the garden as it has been cultivated only since the Sung dynasty. The flowers are esteemed for their intense fragrance. There are several varieties in cultivation, with flowers in various shades of pink, purple, yellow and white. The purple-flowered form is most favored because it is more intensely fragrant than the others.

The Spring Daphne is a shrubby plant. In spring the flowers appear in clusters with the leaves. A very desirable feature of this plant in making arrangements is the pliable nature of the stem. The branches can be bent and twisted to any degree without breaking. Thus they can be freely manipulated to get the desired effect.

Among the relatives of the Spring Daphne are the Genkwa or Lilac Daphne, *Daphne genkwa,* and Edgeworthia, *Edgeworthia chrysantha,* but these flowers are not as showy and fragrant and therefore are less favored in the garden or for arrangement.

51

The Chinese species of Daphne and Edgeworthia are now planted in the warmer regions in Europe and America, but they are not hardy to colder climates.

Hibiscus

Many species of the genus Hibiscus are popular garden flowers in China. It seems, however, that in former times these flowers enjoyed a greater popularity than now. They were very frequently depicted in paintings of the Sung and Ming dynasties and mentioned in poetry and literature. (Plate 19.)

The Chinese Hibiscus, *Hibiscus rosa-sinensis*, is the most common species in China. Double-flowered forms are grown in the garden and appear like roses. The Shrubby Althea, *Hibiscus syriacus*, is less favored and frequently grown as a hedge plant only. The Sunset Hibiscus, *Hibiscus manihot*, is valued not only for its yellow flowers but also for its deeply dissected leaves.

Among these, the Shrubby Althea is now widely planted in western gardens in numerous forms, and is valued chiefly for its late flowering seasons. The Chinese Hibiscus and the Sunset Hibiscus are less hardy and are planted only in warmer regions.

The different species of Hibiscus, although sometimes used as vase flowers, are not preferred plants for this purpose. In the first place, the flowers last for only a very short time. Secondly the stem is usually straight and stiff. However, they are desirable plants because of their autumn flowering habit, when few flowers are in bloom, and also for their relatively large and showy blossoms as well as the attractive foliage.

Foliage

Pines, Bamboos, and Willows are mentioned in the list given by Chang as among the choice materials for classical arrangement. Many conifers are useful in plant arrangement. Pine is the most frequently used, traditionally in association with the Japanese Apricot and Bamboo. Juniper is also a popular decorative plant. (Plates VIC & IXB.)

Among herbaceous plants, the most treasured of all for foliage effect is the Chinese Banana, *Musa basjoo*. It is a plant of southern China with large leaves like the Banana Tree. It can be cultivated in temperate regions of China, though it will not bear flowers as the parts are killed to the ground in winter. The large rich green leaves are most highly valued for their ornamental effect in the garden, especially along walls, among rockeries, or outside windows. A related species called the "Beauty Banana," *Musa uranoscopos*, grows low and is much used in table culture.

An interesting list of foliage plants used to supplement flowers in making arrangements is given in Tu Pêng-tsün's *Monthly Calendar of Vase Flowers* of the early seventeenth century. These plants include both cultivated and wild plants as well as herbaceous and woody ones. He called these plants "little friends of flowers" and arranged them according to the four seasons as follows:

SPRING

| Arrowhead | *Sagittaria sagittifolia* |
| Knotweed | *Polygonum tinctorium* |

SUMMER

Sweetflag	*Acorus gramineus*
"Purple Orchid"	*Bletilla striata*
Mugwort	*Artemisia vulgaris*
Monochoria	*Monochoria korsakowii*
Anise	*Pimpinella anisum*

AUTUMN

Selaginella	*Selaginella uncinata*
Jumpseed	*Tovara filiformis*
Damnacanthus	*Damnacanthus indicus*
Alocasia	*Alocasia macrorhiza*

WINTER

"Wind Orchid"	*Finetia falcata*
Nightshade	*Solanum nigrum*
Kumquat	*Fortunella japonica*

BERRIES

Plants with colorful berries are often used in arrangements. The most popular berry is Nandina or the Heavenly Bamboo, *Nandina domestica,* so called because of its shrubby habit and large pinnately compound leaves with leaflets resembling the foliage of bamboo. The leaves are glossy, richly green and highly decorative. The individual flowers are white and relatively small, but grow in large clusters which develop in late autumn into a mass of showy red berries. These berries are very long lasting and are used extensively in winter for interior decorations. Nandina is now a popular plant in the western garden but it is not completely hardy in the more northern climates. (Plates 15, VIB & X.)

Other ornamental berries or berry-like fruits and seeds include the purple berries of the Beauty Berry, *Callicarpa japonica,* the white berry-like seeds of the Chinese Tallow Tree, *Sapium sebiferum,* the red berries of the Chinese Matrimony Vine, *Lycium chinense,* and many others. These species are now all in cultivation, though not commonly, in western gardens.

LARGE FRUITS AND GOURDS

Some table plants, like Citrus and Pomegranate, are raised for their decorative fruits. These fruits and several others can also be used for table decorations by themselves, in bowls, trays, or baskets, often in association with vase flowers or other table decorations. (Plates 4, 5, 6, 7, 15, 16 & 20.)

Fragrance in Fruit

These ornamental fruits are specially chosen for their interesting shapes or pleasing fragrance, and, above all, for their long lasting quality. The most popular and commonly used ones are Citrons, the Chinese Quince, and the Bottle Gourd.

Citrus medica is a hardy species of Citron that can grow even in the northern part of China. The fruit is oblong, with green to yellow peel which is thick and wrinkled. It is very sour and unfit for eating, but has an intense fragrance and can be kept for a long time. The plant is sometimes also raised as a table plant.

54

Another Citron for table decoration is the celebrated Buddha's Hand, *Citrus sarcodactylus,* sometimes treated botanically also as a variety of *Citrus medica.* The fruit is oblong and yellow, without flesh but with thick rind forming ten to twelve elongated lobes resembling fingers, hence the name. These lobes are natural and not artificially produced. The fruit stays fresh for a very long time and is of intensely pleasing fragrance. It is a very popular decorative fruit and is used all over the country. (Plates 5, 6 & 20.)

The Chinese Quince, *Chaenomeles sinensis,* is a close relative of the Quince and Crab-apple. The tree grows in central and northern China. The fruit is oblong and often of enormous size. It is woody, deep yellow in color and of sweet fragrance, and is unfit for eating when fresh.

The fruit of the Bottle Gourd, *Lagenaria leucantha,* is not fragrant but is valued for its variable and interesting shapes. The fruit is generally elongated and bottle-shaped, and is constricted in the middle. One variety has a large more-rounded fruit, and has been much used as a vessel for holding wines and other things since very ancient times. Others have smaller fruits of various shapes, ranging from flat disc-like to nearly globular, as well as club-shaped, dumbbell-shaped, and coiled or goose-necked. These are generally greenish or tan, but sometimes striped or mottled, and in some cases knobby or ridged. The shells of these fruits are thin but hard and durable, and are used extensively for decorations, as vessels for flowers, and also as containers for medicine. The gourd is of long tradition in folklore. It was an inevitable accessory of many immortals and fairies from which they dispensed beneficial medicine and magic. (Plate 4.)

Among the species of plants mentioned above, the Chinese Quince is now a familiar shrub in western gardens. Though it is mostly grown for its showy flowers, it often bears fruits in quantity. These large peach-like fruits, often beautifully tinged red and green, can be used for interior decorations whenever available. The Buddha's Hand is a warm climate plant, scarcely planted in the west. The Bottle Gourd is also a tender plant, but it has been cultivated in warmer regions all over the world.

55

LING-CHIH FUNGUS

Since very ancient times a woody fungus known as Ling-chih, or the Fomes Fungus, has been treasured as an object of ornamentation and decoration. This is *Polyporus lucidus,* a fungus grown on roots of trees. It is fairly common in the warmer southern parts of China. In the northern part of the country, however, its appearance is very rare and this was considered by the ancient people as a good omen. It was believed that by taking this fungus immortal life could be attained.

The fungus has a stipe and a semi-circular cap which is dark-colored, sometimes tinged with various shades of bright colors, and highly polished like lacquer. It is of hard woody texture and can be preserved in the dried state almost indefinitely. Even when dried and dead, it is frequently placed in pots and trays for table decoration, sometimes in combination with other plant materials. (Plates 4, 20 & XI.)

WEEDS

Many weedy plants can be used effectively in table decorations, especially in groupings of temporary nature. The use of weeds is much preferred by some unorthodox arrangers. Plants like the Dandelion, Plantain, and many others can be used. Some of the foliage plants for arrangement, given in Tu Pên-tsün's list mentioned above, are weedy plants.

Grasses and palms can also be used in the dried state for making arrangements. The most frequently used plant in this condition is the Reed, *Phragmites communis,* whose large panicles of woolly fruits are desirable features in autumn and winter arrangements.

ARTIFICIAL FLOWERS

China is well-known for its artificial flowers, not only because of her skillful handiwork, but also due to the special materials with which these flowers are made to simulate natural ones. The most commonly employed materials are silk cloth and rice paper.

Silk cloths of varying thickness and mesh are used to simulate

Plate VII

Upper: Viburnum. A free arrangement of three floral sprays in a square-bodied blue vase; *lower:* Roses. Three roses arranged in a pink-tinged Peach-blossom vase of the Kang-hsi period.

Plate VIII. LILAC

Two branches of unequal size in a blue square-bodied vase.

Plate IX

Upper: Bleeding-heart. Three floral sprays arranged in a slender neck blue and white Ming vase; *lower:* Maple. A single spray of a cut-leaved variety of Japanese Maple in an archaic white vase of fancy shape.

Plate X. SNOW-BERRY

An American plant that is admirably suited to a Chinese type arrangement.

flower petals of different textures. Silk can also be dyed into any desirable color. Their shiny appearance resembles closely the glossy petals of many flowers and leaves.

Rice paper is a special Chinese product. It is actually a misnomer as it has nothing to do with rice. Actually, it is made of thin slices of the white pith of the Rice Paper Tree, *Tetrapanax papyrifera,* of southern China and Formosa. Large quantities of this paper are produced each year, which go mainly into the making of artificial flowers. The pith is absorbent like blotting paper, of a clear white, slightly dull appearance. It takes color readily and can be made into flowers that do not have petals with a shiny surface.

VII

Table Landscapes

TABLE CULTURE REPRESENTS the culmination of gárden art of China, *the reproduction of idealized landscapes in reduced scale.* Because of the extreme limitation of space, only one or a few plants can be grown in one group. The plants are often the central feature of interest, while the landscape effect is usually reduced to a single piece of stone, and sometimes the judicious use of mosses or weeds for a background or concealing the soil.

Miniature Trees

For the untrained eye, miniature trees often appear grotesque or awkward. They, however, actually represent certain natural features that are much accentuated in Chinese art. The traditional landscapes in Chinese painting, the characteristic precipitous rocky peaks with gnarled pines, are realistic portrayals of some of the scenic mountains in China. Thus, the shapes assumed by most miniature trees are natural, though uncommon, forms that convey best the artistic features in the Chinese sense. *The love of ancient dwarf trees in China is also a manifestation of the great veneration regarding everything that is old.*

Since the plant is the main or only subject of interest, it is treated according to its specific nature in order to bring out its full beauty and to make it a work of art. There is a wide latitude in the selection of material. The best plants are those that are diminutive in size by nature, or those that can be suitably dwarfed. In the latter case, the plants should be able to respond and thrive under the unfavorable conditions of culture which they must endure.

Stem

For miniature trees, the stem is of dominant interest. The texture of the bark is thus an important feature. It is necessary to select the kinds that best portray ruggedness and great age.

The leaves of miniature trees must be relatively small to be in proportion to the size of the plant. By means of dwarfing, these can be often further reduced in size to produce a better effect. Plants selected should be those that can retain the freshness and attractiveness of the foliage under the adverse conditions of treatment, such as, most conifers and maples. *Leaves*

Evergreen plants are often preferred as they are ornamental throughout the year with their foliage on. However, deciduous trees of particular interest and beauty are also used. Many plants are selected for table culture, for their blossoms or fruits. These blossoms are often valued for their striking appearance, but sometimes also for their alluring and pervading fragrance, such as Japanese Apricot.

Aside from some herbaceous plants and a few woody plants that are naturally small in size, the majority of the trees selected for table culture necessitate dwarfing. This process sometimes takes many years. The whole procedure is essentially an art that requires precise knowledge and great patience. Although table plants are produced in quantities by commercial gardeners in China, it is only in the hands of individual plant lovers that the art is brought to its perfection. *Method of Dwarfing*

The principle of dwarfing is to reduce growth activities. However, at the same time the plant must be kept in good physical condition. It is thus important and imperative that a knowledge of the cultural requirements of the particular plant be first acquired. The response to the same treatment may be quite different from one plant to the other. Only those plants that can live and thrive under rather exact conditions will prove useful. Dwarfed trees can be either raised from seeds or from uprooted specimens of desired shapes from the wild.

The basic feature of dwarfed treatment is the confinement of the roots. By growing in a very small container, the roots of a young plant can be trained to grow in a very limited space. Subsequently, the roots are judiciously pruned once every year, or at *Roots* intervals of every two or three years. Sometimes the roots are partially exposed to the air, which reduces their growth and produces a naturalistic effect of old trees clinging to a mountain.

One former author recorded a method practiced by a certain gardener in raising miniature citrus trees. A special container was prepared by using half of a dried orange peel painted on the outside with lacquer. A seedling was planted in this container which was filled with earthworm castings. The whole thing was placed in a flower pot filled with ordinary soil and watered as usual. The small container was lifted up once in a while and any roots that grew out from it were removed by a sharp knife.

In the case of dwarfed specimens transplanted from the wild, it is often necessary to remove these plants with a fair-sized ball of dirt in order to assure their survival. After one or two years, when the plant responds to culture, it is removed to a smaller container with the roots pruned first. This process is repeated again and again until a vessel of the desired size is reached.

It is necessary to limit the amount of nutrient intake of the roots to retard the growth of the plant. The soil is changed only once in two or three years, at which time root pruning is always practiced. Thus, during the dwarfing period the supply of necessary mineral elements, though not entirely withheld from the plant, is kept to a minimum. Water supply is also regulated and much restricted, but it is very important to see that it meets the minimum requirement of the plant.

Branches and Leaves

In addition to treatment of the roots, careful trimming of branches and leaves is practiced for dwarfing purposes. At the same time, the branches are trained to bring the plant into the desired shape. They are often twisted and then tied with wire or twine in order to produce the gnarled effect. Sometimes longitudinal cuts are made to facilitate twisting. The scars, however, should be kept as inconspicuous as possible.

By severe trimming of young branches and foliage, the amount of food produced by the plant by means of photosynthesis is greatly reduced. This naturally results in reduction of the rate of growth of the plant. The total growth of the plant in a given season is correspondingly reduced. The stems thus assume a stunted and venerable appearance, which otherwise would not occur for many more years.

In order to give the plant its desired effect, a definite plan of pruning should be conceived at the very beginning. In trimming a tree, for instance a pine, the leading shoot of each branch, and most of the lateral ones, are removed. The branch thus assumes a new direction of growth, sometimes at right angles to the previous years' growth. The trimming is repeated each year until the branches assume a definite line showing a twisted feature. The combination of the branches into a definite composition will eventually give a wind-swept appearance or other effects. (Plate III.)

Pruning

Various other means are employed to effect dwarfing. Sometimes branches are grafted onto the stem at desired places. The stem can also be tied at various locations to bring out callous formations to enhance the rugged appearance, and to reduce growth by hindering the movement of nutrients.

In the case of flowering or fruiting specimens, the application of fertilizer at the proper moment will bring about the best development of the desired flowers or fruits. Pruning is again important to reduce the amount of vegetative tissues in favor of reproductive ones. The removal of some of the flower buds will bring out fewer but larger and better flowers or fruits.

Table plants require constant and proper care. Long confinement to interior conditions is not congenial to most plants. Neither do the plants long endure shade. However, most table plants, being cramped in a small vessel, will not stand long exposure to direct sunshine. The plants must be taken out into the open for fresh air once in a while, particularly for the benefit of dew in the night. In summertime, they should be protected with bamboo shades during the hottest hours of the day.

Care of Table Plants

Although the basic methods of dwarfing are relatively simple, the fine points of the practical application of these can be obtained only from experience. The basic requirements and responses of

61

the individual species and varieties of plants are different. Only by long and close association with the plants can the technique of growing table plants be brought to perfection.

ON GRAFTING FLOWERS

Red color can be changed into purple
Single flowers can be made double
Small ones can be made large
Few seeds can be made multiple.
"Though Nature bestows fixed characters
I have power to make them change"
He who boasts of his grafting technique
Claims to have taken over Nature's power.
Those who hear this are all astonished
But it often leaves me to sigh
It is indeed clever to use wisdom
But does it really change Nature?
I like to pick chrysanthemums in spring
I like to enjoy peach blossoms in winter
But you cannot plant and graft these
Your cleverness is still in vain.
With rain and dew the grass will grow
With snow and frost the pine still remains
It remains because it has its character
That it grows is also due to the same.
Thus whatever you can change and make
They are all Nature's doing
Nature! Nothing can disobey
What is it that does not follow her?

Ch'en Chuan (Sung Dynasty)

VIII

Plants for Table Decoration

MANY DIFFERENT KINDS of plants, cultivated as well as wild species, are used in making table plants in China. For instance, the book, *Records of Excellent Creations,* of the seventeenth century, states that for table decoration "Pines of Tienmushan rank first among the most ancient trees. The tall ones are not over two feet in height while the shorter ones are about one foot. The trunk is thick like an arm and the needles dense like bundles of arrows. . . . Then there are also old specimens of Mei (Japanese Apricot), thickly covered with mosses. . . . Specimens of Chinese Matrimony Vine, Privet, wild Elm (*Ulmus parvifolia*) and Junipers with snaky stems that do not show scars of tying and cutting, are all valuable ones. Next come the Water Bamboo (*Phyllostachys congesta*) of Hangchow and Damnacanthus (*Damnacanthus indicus*) of Fukien, which are midway between plants of refinement and vulgarity. . . . The Sweetflag, cherished even by the fairies, becomes delicate when grown in rocks and thick when grown in soil, and is very difficult to cultivate. . . . Others like Cymbidium Orchids in spring, Silk Tree, Yellow Fragrant Day Lily (probably *Hemerocallis midden-dorfii*) and Oleander in summer, yellow, dense, dwarfed Chrysanthemums in autumn, and short-leaved Narcissus and 'Beauty Banana' (*Musa uranoscopos*) in winter, can all be made into table decorations according to the season."

The following plants are among those most generally used in table cultures. Some are trees specially adapted for dwarfing. Others are plants of naturally small sizes with certain desired features for use as table plants. Conifers are considered the most ideal plants

63

for dwarfing because of their generally minute evergreen foliage.

Nearly all plants mentioned below have now been introduced into the western garden and are planted either extensively or only occasionally. Species like the Chinese Juniper, Ginkgo, Japanese Maple, Chinese Box, Crape Myrtle, Pomegranate, Chinese Wisteria and many others are among the most widely planted ornamentals in both Europe and North America. Others like Cryptomeria, Golden Larch, Chinese Elm and various species of Azaleas, are also quite extensively planted. The different species of Podocarpus, Bamboos, and Palms are cultivated only in warmer regions or sometimes, such as Podocarpus and the Lady Palm, as greenhouse plants in northern countries.

Besides these Oriental species, similar or related species of plants native to America or Europe can also be adapted for use as dwarf trees. For instance, certain western species of maples, elms, wisterias, larches, pines, etc., can be used for dwarfing like their Oriental relatives. Many other kinds of trees and shrubs, American or European as well as Asiatic in origin, can also be adapted for table culture by dwarfing. It is up to the original and ingenious mind to exploit these unlimited possibilities.

PINES

The Masson Pine, *Pinus massoniana*, the common pine of the hills of southern China, is used to a certain extent as a table plant, but it is not considered ideal for this purpose because of the long needles. The Chinese Pine, *Pinus tabulaeformis*, a closely related species, replaces the former at higher altitudes in central China. It has shorter needles and is more desirable as a table plant.

The Pines, although much grown as table plants, are regarded as rather difficult to handle. Dwarf plants for culture are usually taken from the wild by selecting small plants growing among rock crevices on high mountains, and somewhat stunted and dwarfed by natural adversity. The plants are dug up in the winter when the terminal bud is dominant. The roots should be disturbed as little as possible and with a fair size ball of dirt attached. Then the plants are planted in trays in an effective position to set off the

Plate 9. A BIRTHDAY BASKET

Painting on paper by Prince Yung Jung, sixth son of Emperor
Ch'ien-lung (reign 1736-1796), Ch'ing dynasty. A generous bouquet
of flowers suggesting a wealth of good wishes; baskets instead of
vases are used for such bouquets.

Plates 10-11. THE FOUR SEASONS ON SILK TAPESTRY

K'ang-hsi period (1662-1722), Ch'ing dynasty. From *left* to *right; Spring:* An arrangement of Japanese Plum and Cymbidium in tall vase, also Herbaceous Peony, incense burner, rock and water-pot; *Summer:* Magnolia and Crab-apple behind incense burner, Moutan Peony, Lily and Waterchestnut bulbs, Apples, nuts and jade pieces in foreground. *Autumn:* Osmanthus in tall vase, Sasanqua Camellia in bowl, Chrysanthemum and Bamboo in foreground. *Winter:* Japanese Apricot in tall vase, Nandina in low vase, Narcissus and coins in foreground. Vases are of archaic type.

卉有稱蘭其色紫葉將花
何少香風寡采已見尺山萃
組佩雜糊楚咳克
紫蘭之無不兄用善譜今見此花
間紋色空之以諸花氣而末備上
譽辰院十月御筆

Plate 12. PURPLE ORCHID AND ROCK
Silk tapestry in color, based on a painting by Emperior Ch'ien-lung
(reign 1736-1796), Ch'ing dynasty.

habit and contour. Branches may be trimmed to bring out the best effect.

Most of the pines raised in Chinese gardens come from naturally dwarfed specimens on rocky mountains such as Lushan, Huangshan and Tienmushan in the lower Yangtze valley. These are scenic mountains of great renown. The precipitous peaks and cliffs with arching pine trees and hanging waterfalls are typical landscapes depicted for thousands of years in Chinese paintings. Among these, Huangshan is especially famed for its numerous pine trees which grow everywhere on its rocky slopes. These trees under natural influence assume various weird shapes. Gardeners take great pain in digging up the most desirable specimens and transplanting them into table plants for the market.

As short-leaved species are best suited for dwarfing purposes, the Japanese White Pine, *Pinus parviflora,* is imported from Japan in more recent times for use as table plants.

CRYPTOMERIA

The Peacock Pine or Cryptomeria, *Cryptomeria japonica,* grows into a magnificent tree but it can also be dwarfed as a table plant. The tree has long been cultivated in China with many garden forms. As a miniature tree with its rugged trunk, minute foliage, and small cones it is very ornamental.

In southern China, the Water Pine, *Glyptostrobus pensilis,* is sometimes also dwarfed as a table plant. Its appearance is similar to that of Cryptomeria but it appears more delicate with its more slender stem and foliage.

JUNIPER

The common Chinese Juniper, *Juniperus chinensis,* is much cultivated in the garden as an ornamental plant. It is also frequently used as a pot plant, often in table culture, as the species can be readily dwarfed and the minute foliage is a natural and desirable feature. There are many horticultural forms in cultivation. Some of the varieties are naturally of small stature while still others are procumbent. The foliage is often dimorphic, partly scale-like and partly needle-shaped. The minute foliage of this tree also makes it an ideal plant for topiary work. (Plate IIIC.)

GOLDEN LARCH

The Golden Larch, *Pseudolarix amabilis,* is a deciduous conifer indigenous only to eastern China. It resembles closely the common Larch but has broader and larger leaves. It is a very handsome ornamental tree and is much planted in China. The leaves are yellowish green in spring, turning golden yellow before falling in autumn, hence the name Golden Larch.

The tree is now rare in the wild but is raised from seeds in cultivation. It is by nature a large tree, growing over one hundred feet high, and is of a very graceful habit. It is frequently dwarfed in pots by judicious care from the seedling stage. The scaly red-brown bark adds to the charm of the old miniature trees.

PODOCARPUS

The Yew Podocarpus, *Podocarpus macrophyllus,* is one of the very few species of this largely tropical and subtropical genus that grow in temperate Asia. The plant is frequently grown in pots for topiary work, as it lends itself well to being bent and turned into various shapes.

The garden form generally cultivated is variety *maki,* sometimes called *Podocarpus chinensis,* a smaller form with much smaller leaves. The evergreen leaves are narrow and of rich green. The tree has a natural shapely appearance and can be readily dwarfed for table culture. The bark, which is grayish white and comes off in thick patches, gives the tree an aged appearance.

GINKGO

Ginkgo, the oldest species of all living trees, is preserved in the Chinese gardens and is now a familiar tree in most temperate countries. The tall tree with its naturally straight trunk and branches can be dwarfed and trained into wavy snake patterns. The ease of culture of this tree makes it a suitable one for dwarfing.

Trees thus raised may be only three or four feet high in one or two hundred years.

BAMBOOS

Many species of bamboos are raised for dwarfing purposes as table plants.

In the growth habit, the Chinese bamboos can be grouped naturally into two groups. One group is characterized by the rhizomes, the underground stems, which are long and more slender than the upright culms and indeterminate in their growth. They spread freely in all directions and send up culms at spaced intervals. Another group has rhizomes which are very short and stouter than the upright culms and determinate in their growth. Each one curves abruptly upward at its end to produce a new culm forming in aggregate a dense clump.

The first, which may be referred to as the spreading type, is more common in temperate regions. The second group, which may be referred to as the clump type, is more common in the tropics. These two types of bamboo require different treatments for table culture. The spreading type in general yields to a greater variety of treatment.

A common practice in the dwarfing of the culm of bamboos for table culture is the premature removal of the sheaths which envelop and protect the young shoots. As a result, exposure to light hastens the maturing of the tender young tissue and thus shortens its growth.

The bamboos selected for table culture are mostly those of naturally small or medium stature and those that can be readily dwarfed. Sometimes a large species is also used; the dwarfing in this case is effected by special practice such as mutilation of parts.

The bamboo species native to China are exceedingly numerous. Many are in cultivation for utility purposes or for ornament, a fair number of these being also adapted for table culture. The most commonly used plants are herein listed, with notes on their characteristic features and their culture as table plants. These notes can be adapted for use in many other species of similar nature.

67

Bambusa nana (*Bambusa multiplex*) is a small bamboo with fine foliage, much cultivated in the garden as an ornamental plant. It is of the clump type, forming a dense tuft of shoots. It is called the "Bamboo of Filial Piety" because the young shoots arise in the center of the clump in summer and on the outside in winter, suggesting that the younger generation keeps the older ones cool in summer and warm in winter. By means of dwarfing, this becomes the most popular table bamboo. The small leaves become even more minute after treatment. It is especially suitable for use in making miniature landscape.

Bambusa striata is one of the large bamboos that are sometimes adapted for table culture by special handling. This bamboo, one of the clump type, grows in southern China. It is a much valued ornamental plant because of the unique green and yellow striped stems. In making it into a table plant, a stump with a moderate-sized culm is selected. The top of the latter is cut off in the winter and the clump planted in a flat tray at a slanting position. Large branches arise from the stump in the spring, as well as short vertical shoots from its base. This kind of culture is not of a lasting nature.

A peculiar type of bamboo much esteemed in table culture is called the "Bamboo of the Buddha's Belly," which has greatly shortened but swollen internodes. The successive bulbous stems, frequently irregularly coiled, give the plant a most bizarre appearance. The bulging internodes suggest the round belly of the Laughing Buddha, hence the colloquial name. This is apparently a horticultural form that arises in several species in cultivation. It occurs as a form in *Bambusa ventricosa,* a bamboo of the clump type, and also in *Phyllostachys aurea* of the spreading type. These forms are of naturally small stature and can be further reduced in size by culture.

In central and southern China, there is a common bamboo called the Water Bamboo, *Phyllostachys congesta,* so named because of its preference for damp habitats. It is a dwarf bamboo of the spreading type, of small stature and with fine foliage, and is often used in table culture. This bamboo flowers more frequently than others. *Phyllostachys nigra,* a larger bamboo, is also one of the spreading type but is one that can be readily dwarfed for table culture. The shining black stem is very ornamental. Another bamboo which is often used in table culture is the well known Square Bamboo, *Chimonobambusa quadrangularis*, so named because of its peculiar squarish culm. This bamboo is a native of China only, and is also one of the spreading type. The leaves are slender and of a very graceful appearance.

PALMS

Rhapis, the Lady Palm or the Coir Bamboo, is a small palm peculiar to eastern Asia. Two species of the genus are indigenous to China, both much grown as ornamental plants. *Rhapis humilis* attains a height of four or five feet with the stems, which are not thicker than the thumb, forming a dense clump. *Rhapis flabelliformis* is of smaller stature and with fewer lobes in the leaves. Both palms can be readily dwarfed by cramping the roots and by removing prematurely the sheaths at the base of the leaves. A ten-year-old specimen thus treated may be not more than a foot in height. As table plants they are often grown in flat trays containing miniature rocks. Several stems are allowed to develop from the underground rhizome to give a bushy effect.

The Chusan Palm, *Trachycarpus excelsa*, grows in the warmer parts of China and is the hardiest species of palms in eastern Asia. By nature it attains a height of thirty to forty feet, bearing large palmate leaves. It is much cultivated in the garden and can also be dwarfed for pot culture.

SWEETFLAG

The Chinese Sweetflag, *Acorus gramineus*, is an ornamental plant of long tradition in China. Native to most parts of the country, it grows along streams and usually on rocks, forming great clusters. There are several forms in cultivation which are all smaller than the wild type, the smallest having slender leaves only about an inch or so in length.

For the table, the Sweetflag is used in wet cultures together with rocks. In attaching the plants to suitable rocks the roots are trimmed back severely and the plant bound firmly in the desired position. Then the rocks are submerged partially in water. As new roots are produced, they adhere naturally and the bindings are removed. To dwarf the plant all the leaves are removed once or twice each year.

Lily Turfs

Lily Turfs, plants of the genera *Liriope* and *Ophiopogon,* commonly planted as ground cover or edge plants for their persistent dark green grass-like leaves, originated in China. The flowers, generally lavender in color, are small and borne in a spike. Although the flowers are not showy, they are rather pleasing to the eye. The plants are of easy culture and are raised by dividing the small tuberous roots. They are often used in table cultures, either alone or in association with other plants or dwarfed trees.

The most commonly planted species of this group is *Liriope graminifolia,* called the Book-Tape Herb in China. It is planted in artistically decorated pots, sometimes with rocks, to be placed on the desk of the scholar. Not only the attractive foliage and flowers serve as restful diversion for the eyes, but the numerous slender flat and dryish leaves are exceedingly handy and suitable for use as book-marks.

Rhodea and Reineckia

Rhodea japonica and *Reineckia carnea* are two members of the Lily family, extremely popular as house plants for their ornamental foliage. Both are also often planted in the courtyard or among rockeries in the garden, but more frequently as pot plants and in making table cultures. They have thick perennial rootstocks and persistent foliage. The leaves of Rhodea are very thick, dark green in color and extremely durable, hence it is called the "Ten-Thousand-Year-Green." During the Chinese New Year this is a popular decorative plant for its foliage as well as for the dense clusters of red berries.

Reineckia has narrower, glass-like leaves of a lighter shade. The flowers are not showy, but they are of such infrequent occurrence

70

that the blooming of the plant is considered a good omen for the family, hence it is called the Herb of Felicity. The very presence of this plant around the house is believed to bring good luck to the family. According to former authors, this plant was originally grown in countries to the west of China and was brought to China by the Tartars.

ELMS

Among the several species of Elms in China, the Chinese Elm, *Ulmus parvifolia,* of southern and central China, is the most desirable as a table plant. This Elm is distinguished by its peculiarity in shedding its grayish bark in irregular scaly patches, which gives the trunk an interesting appearance. The foliage is minute and is the smallest among the species of this attractive genus. The branchlets are slender and numerous. In warm temperate regions the leaves are retained through the winter and are shed when new leaves come out in the spring. In the autumn the foliage turns brilliant red and yellow. This species responds well to dwarfing, and altogether is one of the most popular table trees.

The Dwarf Elm, *Ulmus pumila,* of northern to central China, is sometimes also used for table culture. This plant has larger leaves, but there is a pendulous garden form, especially easy for culture, which has hanging twisting branchlets that give the plant a very picturesque appearance.

A relative of the Elms, Zelkova, *Zelkova serrata,* is also commonly used as a table plant. This is a common tree in most parts of China, with foliage and general appearance resembling the Elms, and is treated similarly in making table culture.

MAPLES

Maples are among the most popular table plants. The most commonly used species is the Japanese Maple, *Acer palmatum,* which is a common tree also in eastern China, well-known through the ages for its brilliant red foliage in the autumn. As a garden plant many varieties with different leaf-forms are cultivated. This plant is readily dwarfed for table culture. (Plate IIIB.)

71

Other species of Maples which abound in China are also occasionally used as table plants. For instance, in northern China the species *Acer truncatum* is most commonly planted in the garden and also in table cultures.

BANYAN

The Banyan, *Ficus retusa,* is a huge tree in southern China but it yields itself admirably to dwarfing. The irregular trunk can be trained at will to assume various forms. The trunk and branches send out numerous adventitious roots which enhance its aged appearance. The many branches eventually fuse with the trunk giving the plant its rugged appearance. The evergreen foliage, though thick and relatively large, is rich green and very luxuriant. By dwarfing and successive training, the tree can assume any desired shape. It can be readily trained to attach in part to rocks of any shape, and in various different positions. The underground root system can also be raised partly above ground in many varied patterns without producing any adverse effect on the plant.

BOX

The Chinese Box, *Buxus microphylla,* is a natural favorite for table culture. The tree is evergreen and of very slow growth. The leaves are small and of a rich green texture. In cultivation there is also a naturally diminutive form which can be further dwarfed to be used as a table plant. This tree is much used in making miniature tray gardens, where one or several of these minute trees are planted among rocks to portray mountain scenery.

POMEGRANATE

The Pomegranate, *Punica granatum,* came to China from Central Asia in early times and has since become very much a part of the Chinese garden flora. Many horticultural forms have evolved in cultivation in China. The flaming red flowers and the large reddish fruits are both very ornamental. Dwarfed forms of this plant are highly esteemed as table plants. The stem naturally assumes a crooked and aged appearance. In dwarfing, the leaves also become smaller and are thus in proportion to the size of the plant.

CRAPE MYRTLE

The Crape Myrtle, *Lagerstroemia indica,* is a native of China and is now a familiar garden tree in many parts of the world. It is extensively cultivated in the Chinese garden in many horticultural forms. This is a long-lived tree. Its naturally crooked stem, its shrubby habit, and its ease in culture make it a desirable table plant. The smooth, highly polished, bright satiny barks are very distinctive and delightful. Its delicate and beautiful flowers, blooming continuously for a very long time, are additional charming aspects of this plant.

WISTERIAS

Wisterias are stout woody vines growing to great size and age. The Chinese Wisteria, *Wisteria sinensis,* is much cultivated as an ornamental vine. It can be readily dwarfed for table culture as the roots can stand pruning and cramping when young. The coiled stems, often twisting with each other, can be set in standing or upright positions and shortened by continuous and severe pruning at the top. After a few years of treatment, these upright stems will bear hanging clusters of purplish flowers like a small tree and in a most becoming manner.

The Chinese Wisteria is more suitable for table culture than the Japanese species, *Wisteria floribunda,* because of its much shorter flower clusters. Moreover, all flowers of the clusters open almost simultaneously, instead of gradually down from the top as in the Japanese species, giving it a more floriferous and showy appearance.

AZALEAS

Azaleas are also among the most popular table plants. Their brilliantly colored flowers produced in a long blooming season are great favorites in floral decorations.

Among the Azaleas that are commonly cultivated in the Chinese garden are the red-flowered Indian Azalea, *Rhododendron simsii,* the purple-flowered Lovely Azalea, *Rhododendron pulchrum,* the yellow-flowered Chinese Azalea, *Rhododendron molle,* and the white-flowered Snow Azalea, *Rhododendron mucronatum.* These plants are frequently used as pot plants and are often dwarfed for table culture.

The twiggy habit of most species of Azaleas does not lend itself well to treatment as dwarf plants. Only by long care and careful trimming can desirable plants with rugged features be secured.

Frequently, plants dwarfed by adverse conditions in the wild are used for table culture. Some of the species mentioned above are very common plants in the hills of central China where they grow among rocks and in thickets. The shrubbery of these hills is constantly being cut for use as fuel. As a result, Azalea plants with roots buried deep among the rocks often attain great age but with only a short and stout stump above the ground. These stumps, angular and gnarled on account of repeated mutilations through many years, often exhibit remarkably well the desired artistic features of Chinese pictorial art. Gardeners dig up these stumps, as well as similarly dwarfed trees of other kinds, for culture in trays. Even though a relatively small proportion of the transplanted plants may eventually survive in culture, the high prices commanded by choice specimens well compensate the effort. A dwarf stump of Azalea of apparent great age, setting off a few small branches with brilliantly colored flowers, is a pleasing sight.

On a Potted Pomegranate in Flower

A spot of red on top of a small tree,
  Smiling in the Lotus breeze of the sixth moon;
Among the green foliage hides a coral blossom,
  As if silver is placed in a golden blue bush.

Emperor K'ang-hsi (reign, 1662-1722)

IX

Vases, Pots and Trays

THE MOST IMPORTANT vessels used for flower arrangement in China are of bronze and porcelain. The floral art of China is undoubtedly greatly aided and stimulated by the highly developed crafts of pottery and porcelain, of which China is justifiably famous. Many other wares of lesser importance are also used, such as lacquer, cloisonné, glass, marble, and bamboo.

The selection of appropriate receptacles for arrangement is a matter of careful deliberation. The choice has to be considered in respect to the plant, the season, the location, the occasion, and the setting.

Chang Ch'ien-tê, as translated in Appendix I, speaks most authoritatively on the subject of selecting receptacles for flower arrangement. Writing in the same period, Yüan Hung-tao stressed similarly the importance of selecting the best containers for flowers. He writes:

Chang Ch'ien-te Advises

"I have seen ancient bronze Ku as heirlooms in families of Kiang-nan, deeply impregnated with blue and green and mottled with grit, golden dwellings, indeed, of flowers. Next come ceramic wares like Kuan, Ko, Hsiang and Ting, elegant, enticing, lustrous and glamorous, exquisite abodes, too, of the spirit of the flowers.

"In general, vases of the study should be low and small, such as flower Ku, bronze Chih, Ts'un, Lei, square Han Hu and flat Hu among the bronze wares; and paper-beater vase, goose-necked vase, eggplant pouch, flower Ts'un, flower bag, yarrow and cattail mace among the ceramic wares. Only those of small and short statures are eligible for elegant decoration, otherwise they may appear like

75

offerings in the temple; and even though they are ancient, they look vulgar. However, flowers are of different sizes. Large massive flowers like Moutan Peony, Herbaceous Peony and Lotus do not fall into this limit."

Bronze Containers

In ancient times, bronze was used extensively. The most beautiful and artistic productions were made by the Shang people, about the twelfth to the eighteenth centuries B.C. Many similar bronze vessels of great variety of shapes were also executed at later ages, down to the Han dynasty. Among them were vessels of all kinds for ceremonial uses and for holding wine and cereals. These precious art subjects, frequently excavated from the ground in later times, are much sought by art collectors and are used sometimes as containers for flower arrangement. The green patina formed by chemical reactions in the soil adds much to the charm and beauty of these ancient wares.

These ancient bronze vessels have never been surpassed in their beauty of craftsmanship and design. The bronze employed is an alloy consisting, according to modern analysis, of about eight or nine parts of copper and one part of tin, with small amounts of some other metals added. They are often embellished with art designs or inscriptions and are made in a great variety of shapes. Those vases and jars, mentioned by Chang and Yüan, for use originally as wine goblets, adapt admirably well to flower arrangement. The simplest and most beautiful vessel is the Ku, a drinking vessel which is a tall and slender cylindrical vase with a hollow base, a slightly expanding body, and trumpet mouth. Another, the Ts'un, is very similar in shape but usually broader and heavier. It occurs in a cylindrical and squarish form. The Hu is a wine container, shorter and heavier, with broad bulbous body and slender neck, and has a lid covering the top. There are two handles ("ears"), which are sometimes appended with two rings. What was called P'ing of the period of the "Spring and Autumn Annals" (722-481 B.C.) is a type of Hu. Lei is a larger container, much heavier and broader than Hu and with a very short neck. The shapes of these elegant vases ought to delight and inspire the modern designer and arranger. (Figures 7 & 8.)

76

Antiques and curios are, however, not available to every one. There are thus imitations of ancient bronze offered by art dealers. These wares are frequently also buried in the ground for some time to acquire the darkened and worn out effect of ancient wares. New bronze vases of more modern designs are also made for flower arrangements.

Pottery in China developed since prehistoric times. Gradually, the technique became refined, and translucent and resonant porcelain was developed. True Chinese porcelain was known at least around the eighth century in the T'ang dynasty. It is also during this period that floral art became popular.

The Sung ceramic wares, of the tenth to the thirteenth centuries, are among the finest ever made, showing great achievement in taste, refinement, and technical skill of the potters. These are in general porcelaneous in nature, that is, white or translucent or highly vitrified like porcelain. Various types are now recognized and can be identified, among which are some that were designed specially for use in flower art. These Sung wares and wares of the later Ming dynasty are among those mentioned by Chang and Yüan. (Plate XII, Figures 7 & 8.)

Sung Ceramics

Some of these early wares of Sung were scarcely preserved to this day. While the generally recognized types can be easily identified, certain kinds such as the imperial wares like Ch'ai (named after the ruling family Ch'ai) of the pre-Sung Chou period (951-960), and Ju (named after Juchow), and Kuan (official) types of the Sung period have been tentatively identified only in recent years and their exact nature is uncertain.

There are several more well-known types of Sung wares, generally accepted, such as Lung-chüan, Chün, Chien and Ting. The most famous is the Lung-chüan type, known in the west as celadon, named after the district in Chekiang province which was the main center of manufacture. The glaze is of sea-green in various beautiful tones. This ware is thick and heavy, and was exported in large quantities. It is found all over the world and was already greatly treasured in Europe and the Near East in Medieval times. The

Celadon

ware was continuously manufactured during the Yüan and Ming dynasties, and in later times.

There were two brothers of the Chang family working separately at Lung-chüan. The elder brother (Shêng-i) distinguished his productions by calling them Ko ware, meaning elder brother. The young brother (Shêng-êrh) continued the old Lung-chüan style, and his ware was known as Chang ware or Chang Lung-chüan ware. This ware was called Chang-shêng by Chang Ch'ien-tê.

Another kind of famous ware is Chün ware, originally made at Chün-chou in Honan province. The glaze is of the most exquisite color, ranging from deep purple to sky blue. These vessels were mostly broad and shallow for use as flower pots and bulb bowls, supplying the imperial court. These wares were also made in the Yüan and Ming dynasties and were freely imitated in later times.

Still another kind of Sung ware is the Chien type, named after the town in Fukien province where the center of manufacturing was located. The type has a heavy strong body covered by a thick black glaze streaked with gold and silvery markings. Among these is a ware called Wu-ni (Black Earth) which was made in Chien-an.

Another type of famous ware, called Ting ware, was produced in Ting-chou in Hopei province. This is a true porcelain in every respect. It is usually white and is beautifully decorated with incised or moulded designs over the surface. These decorations, usually in the form of birds or flowers, were delicately and exquisitely drawn like fine paintings. These wares were made all over China in subsequent years and thus vary greatly in quality.

A type of less known ware, called Hsiang ware, was made after the Sungs moved south in 1127. Its origin is unknown but is believed generally to be Hsiang-shan of Chekiang province. This ware looks like Ting, but with heavier body.

Ming Porcelains

During the Ming dynasty, a period of wealth and splendor, porcelain manufacture, under imperial patronage, reached its full flower, showing the greatest artistic originality. The center of production was Ching-tê Chen in Kiangsi province in central China, since then known all over the world where the best porcelains are produced up to this day.

78

While the Sung wares were largely monochrome, during the Ming period multicolored and painted porcelains were greatly preferred. The paintings were done in enamel colors or in blue. The largest group were the well known blue and white ones, of porcelain with underglaze painting in cobalt blue. The designs were ornamental or pictorial, representing flowers, birds, legendary figures, or scenes of everyday life. A less frequently used color was copper red. (Plates 17, IX & XIV; Figures 8-10.)

The multicolored porcelains of the Ming period belong to two groups, the so-called three-colored and five-colored wares, although the colors were not strictly three or five. The three-colored glaze was applied strictly to the body, while in the five-colored type the enamel was generally applied to the glaze and not to the unglazed body.

The best porcelains of the Ming dynasty were produced during the reigns of Hsüan-tê (1426-1435) and Ch'êng-hua (1465-1487), and are known as the Hsüan and Ch'êng wares respectively. Original pieces of these wares are now comparatively rare. Among the Hsüan wares the blue and white ones are considered the best, while in the Ch'êng wares the five-colored ones are most famous.

Many of the exquisite types of the Sung and Ming porcelain were continuously made in later periods or were freely imitated. In the Ch'ing dynasty, during the long reign of the emperor K'ang-hsi (1662-1722), porcelains were produced which equal the finest wares of the Sung period. Famous wares were also produced in the reigns of Yung-chêng (1723-1735) and Ch'ien-lung (1736-1796).

In the Ch'ing dynasty, the kilns at Ching-tê Chen were restored and expanded. New shapes and designs, as well as new colors and glaze, were developed. Besides their domestic usage, Chinese porcelains now enjoyed great popularity in western countries. Many works of these reigns were produced for export to the foreign market.

The porcelains of the Ch'ing dynasty fell into three main types. The first type was the blue and white ware continuing the Ming tradition. The decorations were often of flowers, such as the popular Peonies, Japanese Apricot, Lotus, Chrysanthemum, and many

Ch'ing Wares

others. The second type was ware decorated with transparent enamels like those of the Ming period. The colors were similar but the designs more variable, and often more elegant. These were ornamental in nature, showing birds, flowers, and legendary scenes. The third group was monochromes, following the Sung ware. The colors used were red, pink, black, blue, green, pale lavender, and others, often in exquisite shades. (Figures 9 & 10.)

In the latter years of the Ch'ing dynasty the art of porcelain, as well as the other arts, gradually declined, and the productions, while often showing fine workmanship and great technical skill, seemed to lack the vigor and beauty of the work of the former eras.

For Sixteenth and Seventeenth Century Arrangers

The quotations from the works of Chang and Yüan show that flower arrangers of the sixteenth century were very particular in their choice of the shape and form of vases. The book, *Records of Excellent Creations,* by Wen Chêng-hêng, written in the early seventeenth century, describes, among other things, choice porcelain wares for various purposes. On vases for flower arrangement, the book mentions Kuan, Ko and Ting wares, in the shape of gall bladder vases, single-twig vases, little yarrow vases, and paper-beater vases as among the choicest vessels. Others like eggplant pouch, gourd-like vases, vases with hidden decorations, blue and white vases, and slender legged medicine jars were less desired. Goose-necked wall vases were considered even more inelegant. The book mentions also that some of the large Lung-chüan and Chün wares of a height of two or three feet were suitable for arranging large old boughs of the Japanese Apricot flowers, and that it was desirable to use tin tubes in flower vases in winter to prevent cracking.

These statements are very similar to those given by Chang Ch'ien-tê. This shows either that they were based on Chang's slightly earlier authoritative statements, or that the views expressed by these authors were the generally recognized and prevalent ones of that period.

In recent times, although Chinese porcelain wares have been extensively and intensively studied by specialists and connoisseurs all over the world, and the different wares are fairly well known

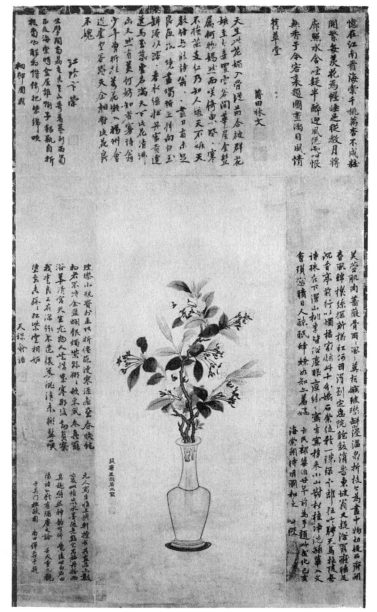

Plate 13. CRAB-APPLE IN A GLASS VASE

Painting in ink on paper by Wang Yuan-shih (14th century), one
of the greatest painters of the Yuan dynasty. The writings are poems
or essays composed by scholars and painters in praise of the painting. This simple arrangement of a popular flower is an excellent
example of rhythmic vitality so important in work with flowers.

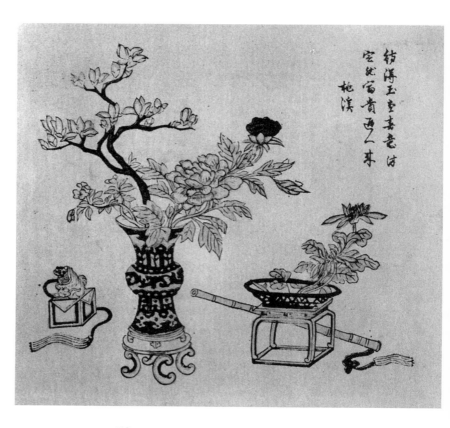

Plate 14. SPRING DECORATIONS

Colored woodblock print, 18th century. Magnolia, Crab-apple and Moutan Peony
in tall vase form a rebus *Yü Tang Fu Kuei,* "Wealth and honor in halls of jade."
Other decorations are a stone seal, a flute and a basket of Chrysanthemums.

Plate 15. NEW YEAR'S DECORATIONS

Colored woodblock print, 18th century. Camellia, Nandina and Japanese Apricot
in tall vase with a handsome bowl of well-arranged fruits, a book and a carved *ju-i*
handle, an auspicious symbol shaped like the Ling-chih Fungus.

Plate 16. AN ARRANGEMENT OF FRUITS
Colored woodblock print, 17th century. Apples and Pomegranates,
both felicitous fruits, in a porcelain bowl on a lacquer stand.

as to their origins and nature, little work has been done to eluci-
date on the various shapes and forms of these wares and their
specific usage.

As mentioned above, the authors of the sixteenth and seventeenth   *Sources of*
centuries were very specific in their choice of the desirable forms of   *Diagrams*
vase for arrangement. The identification of these various forms
is not only of historical significance in Chinese art, but is also of
direct interest to students of the classical type of flower arrangement
in China. In the Palace Museum of Peking, where the imperial
collections are preserved, there are records of all porcelain wares
bearing descriptive names. The diagrammatic illustrations given
here are based on published works dealing with authentic specimens
of the Museum.

The earlier porcelain wares, such as a few of the Sung dynasty
still extant, were patterned after ancient pottery and bronze ceremonial vessels. These were often of austere forms, sometimes circular and sometimes angular. Later on, the designs were more
practical, tended to be mostly roundish, and were gay and secular.

Fig. 7. Types of Sung vases patterned after ancient ritual vessels.
From left to right: Ku, Ts'un, Hu.

In a work entitled *T'ai Yueh T'u Sho* undertaken by imperial
command and published in 1743, T'ang Ying, the celebrated super-
intendent of the Ching-tê Chen potters in the eighteenth century,

81

explained in flowery language in the form of comments on twenty illustrations showing the processes of porcelain manufacture, the origin and differentiation of these two main types of designs. Pieces of the first type, patterned after ancient ceremonial wares such as Ts'un, Ku and Hu, were called "Cho" or "Ornamental" pieces. These have a variety of shapes: square, circular, and angular. Gradually, these archaic styles of the past were replaced in later times by "Yüan" or "Round" pieces, such as vases and other pieces like bowls, cups, plates, and dishes of modern design.

Ritual Vessels

Among the shapes of ritual vessels modeled for use as flower vases are wine vessels like Ts'un, Ku, and Hu described under bronze wares above. The earlier ones were decorated with ornamental patterns similar to those of the ancient wares. Vessels modeled after Hu often had two handles (or ears), and sometimes from these handles were appended rings duplicating those of the ancient wares. (Plates 10, 11 & Figure 7.)

These handles were later often adopted for attaching tapes for hanging on walls. These were hollow and were called "piercing ears." The vases modeled after Ku were all rounded, while those modeled after Hu came in different shapes, such as square, flattened, hexagonal, and octagonal. Later on, modified vases frequently had only remnants of the handles, while in others the handles were entirely absent. Those with wide mouths were also known as two-tubed vases, as two tin tubes could be inserted into each vase.

A kind of elongated square vessel called Ts'ung-shaped vase was modeled after a yellow jade piece called Ts'ung, used in ancient times for worshiping of earth. All these different kinds of vases of the Sung period patterned after ancient ceremonial vessels were imitated and reproduced in later periods.

Flower vases of later periods, including those that are still in common usage up to the present, are derived from these archaic styles. From Ts'un and Hu are derived variously shaped vessels called Hua Nang or flower bag, and Hua Cha or flower receptacles. Among the first are usually short and stout vessels, some with vestiges of the handles and some without. The latter is a

82

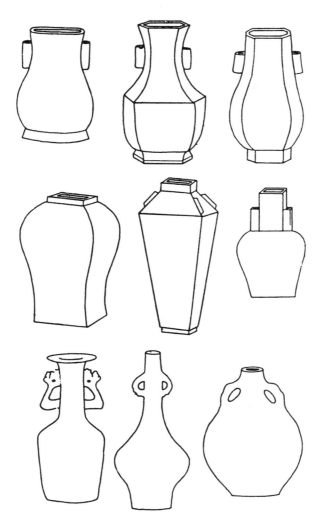

Fig. 8. Types of Sung and Ming vases derived from
ancient ritual vessels.

From left to right, first row: double-tubed vase with piercing ears, hexagonal
vase with piercing ears, octagonal vase with piercing ears; *second row:* square
vase, flattened square vase, three-spouted flattened square vase; *third row:*
phoenix-eared vase, elephant-eared vase, bow-eared flattened vase.

collective name for vessels of miscellaneous shapes that can be used for holding flowers. There are also elongated or tubular vessels that can be used both for arranging flowers and holding brush-pens. These tubular vessels are especially adapted for use with erect straight branches of flower stalks such as Iris and grasses.

True Vases
Vessels of the true vase type are also variable in their shape. A most common form, prevalent since Sung, is called Tan P'ing, a vase shaped like a gall bladder. Later the name is more generally applied to vases with straight necks, while those with gradually expanded mouth are commonly known as Yü-hu-ch'un. The long slender-necked ones are called goose-necked vases. Those with bulbous mouth are called Wen Hu, as they resemble the hot water bottle. (Figure 9.)

A kind of vase with a baluster body is called Kuan-yin P'ing, because it is shaped like the vase held by Kuan-yin, the Lord of Mercy. Another common vase with a similar type of body, but with a very short neck and small mouth, is generally called Mei P'ing or Japanese Apricot (Mei) vase. This type is also known as one-twig vase because the small mouth is designed for holding a single twig, particularly that of the Japanese Apricot. (Figure 9.)

These are among the more generally used kinds of flower vases up to the present time. Aside from Mei P'ing, they can be used for all types of flower arrangements. The selection of flowers and matching vases is determined mainly by their relative size.

The other more or less standard shapes, but of less common usage, include Lai-fu P'ing or turnip vase, Chi-ch'ui P'ing or paper-beater vase, Pi-ch'i P'ing or water chestnut vase, and Pu-chui P'ing or cattail mace vase, all so named because of their respective shapes resembling these various objects.

The use of these vases is again determined by the relation of their size to the size of the branches of the flowers. In general, large flowers such as Peonies demand large vessels. Likewise, large branches of small flowers, such as Japanese Apricot or Wintersweet, also require large vases.

There are also other kinds of vases of fancier shapes. A common type of vase is shaped like the gourd Hu-lu and called Hu-lu P'ing.

84

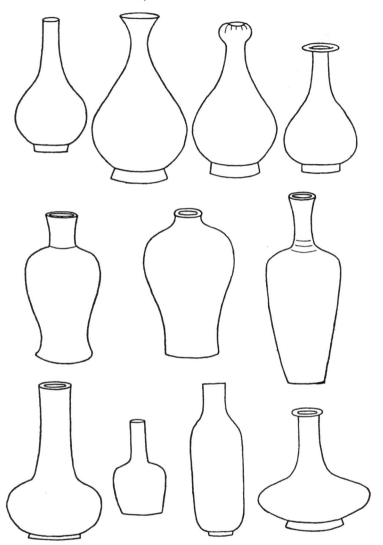

Fig. 9. Types of conventional Ming and Ch'ing vases.

From left to right, first row: gall vase, Yü-hu-ch'un vase, hot water bottle vase, flanked-mouthed goose-necked vase; *second row:* Kuan-yin vase, one-twig vase, turnip vase; *third row:* water-chestnut vase, paper-beater vase, cattail mace vase, long-necked flat vase.

85

Vases of Fancy Shape

There are also those with flattened bodies called Pien Hu, or flat vase or pot. Flat vases with handles are often used against pillars or walls for hanging or drooping arrangements.

Among the other fancier kinds are one called Shang-lien P'ing, or double vase, which has two vases of the same size and shape joined side by side. One of these is called San-chieh P'ing, or three-tiered vase, having three stories like a pagoda; the other, Pao-chu Hua-cha, a flower receptacle in the shape of a firecracker, made of bamboo. These fancier types are also usable for various types of arrangements, according to their sizes, like the other vases mentioned above, but they are generally not considered in good taste for use in making arrangements by the more discriminating arranger. (Figure 10.)

For table cultures, there are pots or trays, either in pottery or porcelain. Flower pots of China are among the handsomest of all countries. They are generally shaped like a bowl, some high and some low. These are either unglazed or glazed, and are either in solid colors or embellished with decorations of flowers or birds, or with well-known verses. (Figure 11.)

Special Flower Pots

These pots are also made in many patterns. They are sometimes specially prepared and designed for use with specific plants such as Cymbidium Orchids. These flower pots all have large holes at the bottom for drainage, and are often placed on a matching dish.

According to the book, *Records of Excellent Creations,* of the seventeenth century: "The best flower pots are those of green or ancient bronze and ceramic wares of the kilns Ting, Kuan, Ku, etc. Among the new wares, those like five-colored imperial wares and 'spring-borrowing' rough wares can also be used. The rest are not eligible. The pots should be round and not squarish, while the narrow elongate ones are especially undesirable."

In selecting pots for use, they should be of a shape or color harmonious to the plant. Connoisseurs generally prefer those of individual design. A highly ornate pot is not in favor lest it distract the attention from the plant, which is the primary object.

Flat trays are used for the type of culture where rocks are used to enhance the landscaping effect. These trays were generally of ob-

86

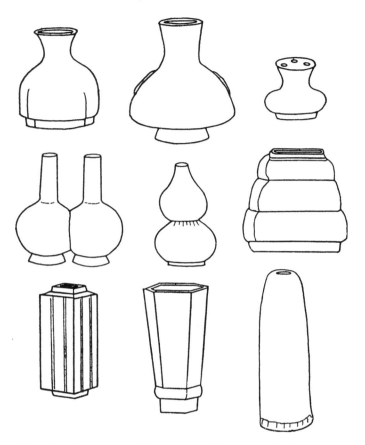

Fig. 10. Some special types of Ming and Ch'ing vases.

From left to right, first row: flower bag, straight-necked flower bag, three-spouted little flower receptacle; *second row:* double vase, gourd vase, three-tiered vase; *third row:* Ts'ung-shaped vase, flower receptacle, bamboo fire-cracker-shaped flower receptacle.

long shape, with or without holes in the bottom, for dry or wet cultures, respectively. Trays carved out of white marble are also used for the latter purpose. But on the whole, plain, simple earthenware trays are usually preferred as a setting for either plant or landscaping cultures. The culture of Narcissus is made in a special kind of shallow bowl. (Figure 11.)

Trays for Land- scapes

87

The culture of Lotus also calls for a special kind of vessel. This is a large round bowl of earthenware, decorated on the outside with glazed design of the Lotus.

Stands

All kinds of vases and trays are usually supported on a specially made matching stand or small table. These are generally made of highly polished wood in "mahogany" finish. They are of various designs and of different heights, for placing either on the floor or upon tables in different parts of the room. (Plate IV.)

Besides bronze and porcelain, other makes of vases include lacquer, glass, cloisonné, and also silver, although the use of the latter is not considered refined except for special occasions, such as wedding ceremonies.

Lacquer Wares

Lacquer is another contribution of China. Its early history is little known and it must have originated at the dawn of Chinese history. Lacquer wares have now been discovered which date back to the Chou dynasty. In the T'ang and Sung dynasties, lacquer manufacturing was already very advanced, while the best wares were produced in the Ming dynasty.

There are generally two types of lacquer wares, flat painted ones and carved ones. The best painted works were produced in southern China, especially in Foochow and Canton. The finest carved work was prepared in Peking in nothern China, and Soochow in eastern China. There are many articles made of lacquer such as screens, vases, trays, and numerous others. Lacquer vases generally follow the conventional shapes of porcelain ones. The making of fine lacquer wares, both flat and carved, is an elaborate process. Many layers are required for each piece. A carved piece, for instance, may take years to prepare and then years to carve.

A special kind of vessel is made out of bamboo tubes. These tubes can be carved into all possible forms. The naturally glossy surface of bamboo can be utilized for carving out decorations such as a picture or a verse. Gourds are sometimes also used as flower vases. Vases made of split bamboos, with a bamboo tube placed inside for water, are made in some parts of the country.

The use of some specially designed baskets for flower arrangement may be claimed as another Chinese innovation. Since very

Plate XI. LING-CHIH FUNGUS
Several specimens planted in gravel in a flower pot.

Plate XII. BULB BOWLS AND FLOWER POTS
OF THE SUNG DYNASTY
(Percival David Foundation, London); *upper:* Crackle Kuan ware, bulb bowls;
lower: Chun ware, flower pots with drain holes.

Plate XIII. FLOWER BASKETS
Old Chinese flower baskets of **bamboo (From** *Chinese Baskets* by H. Laufer)

Plate XIV. BLUE AND WHITE VASES
OF THE MING DYNASTY

(Freer Gallery of Art). *Upper left:* Flat vase; *upper right:* Gourd-shaped vase;
lower left: Kuan-type vase; *lower right:* Mei P'ing or one-twig vase.

Plate XV. ACCESSORIES FOR FLOWER ARRANGEMENT
Upper left: Bronze incense burner; *upper right:* Carved jade; *lower left:* Carved
wooden figure; *lower right:* Carved ivory brush holder.

Plate XVI
Carved jade mountain (Cleveland Museum of Art—Worcester R. Warner Collection)

Fig. 11. Types of flower pots and bulb bowls.

early times baskets have been extensively used by the Chinese for all purposes. In ancient times baskets were used as ceremonial vessels, as containers for storing food and other articles, and in carrying out the work of the farmers. They were made with bamboo strips, straw, willow twigs, or wood. Later on, basketry became a highly developed craft and baskets were often beautifully lacquered or painted, or sometimes embellished with metals. (Plates 8, 18, 19 & VIII.)

Baskets   Flower baskets were apparently developed in the T'ang dynasty, or earlier, along the Yangtze valley. They are now used by street vendors of flowers and for making interior arrangements and decorations. They come in a great variety of design, often delicately woven in elegant shapes with graceful handles. They deserve the serious consideration of the modern designer and the art student.

X
Rocks and Other Accessories

THE USE OF ROCKS in connection with table plants and flower decoration is *a unique feature of the floral art of China.* When appropriately used with certain plants and flowers, rocks can be an attractive adjunct, enhancing artistic effects. (Plates 12 & VIA.)

The use of rocks in interior decorations apparently stemmed from the rockery in the Chinese garden. The typical Chinese garden is made up to a large extent by rock works, on which the charm of the garden usually depends. The craze for artificial rock hills in China has no equal in the whole world.

The artistic grouping of stones in gardens seems to go back to very early times in China. Records show that rock gardens were in existence as early as the Han dynasty (206 B.C.-220 A.D.). The first extensive garden devoted to this artistry was built by Emperor Huei-tsung (reign 1101-1125) of the Sung dynasty, one of the greatest artists in Chinese history. The imperial rock commissioner was sent far and wide in search of suitable stones for the garden. The most treasured rocks came from Lake Tai in eastern China. Stones from the bottom of the lake were carried by barges through thousands of miles to the capital Kaifeng in northern China. The craze for Tai-hu rocks reached its height during the latter part of the Ming dynasty in about the sixteenth century. Fabulous prices were paid for the most fantastically shaped pieces.

Tai-hu rocks are at present still the most treasured and desired for the garden. These rocks, now laid at the bottom of the lake, were pounded in former times through thousands of years of ocean

Tai-hu Rocks

91

waves. Through scouring and washing by water, they become porous and grotesque, assuming fantastic shapes. They are often twisted, furrowed, and deeply and profusely perforated. Similar stones from other regions are also used, thought often of much less value.

Pleasure in Stones

This enthusiasm for rocks is probably also the result of the Chinese landscape itself, as in many parts of China the mountains and gorges are often unbelievably grotesque. The passionate love of Chinese artists for rockery is purely artistic, and is not worship as claimed by some authors. History records one artist so fond of rock as to pay homage at a great distance to a very strange looking rock. Another hailed one stone as his brother. Now, as before, fantastically shaped stones in gardens are often designated with fanciful names, and credited with sentiments and moral qualities. These are all just expressions of profound appreciation, for when a stone is endowed with personality it becomes a delightful companion.

Thus, stones and rockery, besides being of attractive appearance, assume also symbolic meanings. Stones have in general the quality of permanence and solidity. These are characteristics which by comparison, make men feel humble because they are ephemeral and changeable.

In another way, the presence of stones in gardens serves as a bridge linking plant life with buildings. It acts as a natural transition between nature and human creations.

Thus stones are found in all Chinese gardens, large and small. No Chinese garden is without rockery and sometimes the rock hill dominates the entire garden. It is natural that in a miniature tray garden, which is a derivation of landscape gardening, the original dominant feature is also a piece of rock.

Miniature Gardens

From old paintings and prints, it is evident that stone was the dominant feature in the early miniature gardens. A piece of stone, placed in a tray of water, with some small plants growing along the edge and among the crevices, apparently suggested to the early artists the idea of an island where the legendary immortals lived.

92

This scene was frequently depicted in ancient paintings. (Plate XVI.)

The early use of rock in the miniature tray garden was thus derived from the Chinese garden scenery, with rockeries artificially constructed in a garden lake. The earliest records of this kind of garden scene date back to the second century B.C. The scene was based on a belief in the magic isles of the immortals, which lay in the eastern oceans, a part of the earliest Chinese folklore.

The dwarfing of trees for planting with stones was apparently an idea developed much later. Through the ages, as the art of dwarf trees became more and more popular, these trees were also planted by themselves as the chief object, without stones. But stones as art objects persist to the present time. (Plates 12 & VIA.)

In recent times, besides miniature landscapes with stones and *Stones on* dwarf trees, artistically shaped stones are still considered suffi- *Pedestals* ciently interesting in themselves to be used as a decorative feature. These stones are placed on a pedestal and used alone, or more frequently in combination with table plants, vase flowers, or other table decorations. These curious rock forms are so greatly prized that they are handed down in families as precious heirlooms.

As stones used for interior decorations are of much smaller size than rockeries for the garden, emphasis is also laid on the color, texture, grain, and other fine qualities. Different degrees of translucence and shades of color are of great importance. The finer details are often only perceptible to the experts.

Mei Fei, the great painter of the Sung dynasty and a great lover *Mei Fei* of rocks, gave four criteria for judging rocks, namely, *delicacy,* *Judges* *wrinkle, clarity, and slenderness.* Another Sung author Tu Wan, wrote a special treatise on rocks called *Yün Lin Shih Pu,* enumerating over a hundred different kinds of rocks and recording their origins and characteristics. These were mainly rocks from a few inches to one or two feet in height, for use as table decorations. Some of the larger rocks described were also used for making finer rock works in the garden.

Besides stones, other accessories for table decorations include

Feather and Other Accessories

plumes, table screens, incense tripods, figurines, corals, and other antiques and curios. The most frequently used plume is peacock feather. The large brilliantly colored tail feathers, with a prominent "eye" on each, are very decorative and were used in imperial times as an insignia of high official rank. They came to China regularly as part of the required tribute from Annam and other countries in the south. The peacock has long been a symbol of splendor in China. In former times the feathers were also conferred on officials by the emperors as reward for merit, to be worn on hats. (Plate XV.)

There is also other decorative plumage, such as the brilliantly colored long pointed tail feathers of the golden Manchurian pheasants, and the white feathers of the egret. The latter are often dyed red or blue.

Table Screens and Corals

Table screens are made of marble, jade, porcelain, and other materials, supported by a delicately carved wooden frame. The more precious forms of corals, especially the profusely branched red ones, are used for decorations, either alone and mounted on stands, or with plants in cultures. They are called "Coral Trees." Bronze or porcelain incense tripods, and figurines of these or other materials, as well as curios and antiques of all kinds, can be used in accordance with the originality and taste of the owner.

XI

Enjoyment of Flowers

THERE IS SOME difference in the enjoyment of flowers between the East and the West. *According to the western approach to life, man is the dominant element,* while flowers, birds, animals, and the natural scenery in general form a background for his enjoyment. Man is the lord and ruler of creation, and everything else is there to serve him when needed.

In China, man and plant are considered on equal terms. And man has much to admire and learn from plants, for they seem to partake of a more ideal existence. Their exhilarating growth, aspiration for light, regularity of appearance, their beauty and charm, their purity and sweetness, are all appealing qualities.

Eastern and Western Approaches

Flowers should be best enjoyed in their natural habitat. As Yüan Hung-tao noted, the enjoyment of vase flowers is just a substitute for people living in the cities who must forsake happiness of enjoying the natural sceneries. Thus, when it is necessary to pick flowers and arrange them in vases, *it has to be done with humility and compassion.* Only by tending them with the best care and providing them with a suitable background can one enjoy the real beauty of the flowers.

Therefore the Chinese practice is to prescribe the proper moment and surroundings for enjoying a thing. The very atmosphere is the essence of enjoyment. This is true in many things that one can enjoy in life, among which flower is one of the most attractive.

Among the works of earlier authors who discoursed on this subject, perhaps the best is the thesis on the enjoyment of the Mei flower (Japanese Apricot) by Chang Ts'u. Chang is an author of

95

Enjoyment of the Japanese Apricot

the twelfth century in the Sung dynasty. His famous treatise on the Japanese Apricot lists the following twenty-six conditions as suitable to the enjoyment of this most beloved flower.

1. Thin clouds
2. Morning sun
3. Slight chill
4. Drizzling rain
5. Light smoke
6. Clear moon
7. Setting sun
8. Light snow
9. Evening sky
10. Precious birds
11. Lone crane
12. Crystal stream
13. Small bridge
14. Edge of bamboos
15. Shade of pines
16. Bright window
17. Sparse hedge
18. Rugged rocks
19. Green mosses
20. Bronze jar
21. Paper screen
22. Flute in the woods
23. Chin (lute) on the knees
24. Playing chess on a stone board
25. Brewing tea and sweeping snow
26. A beauty plainly dressed and wearing a bamboo hat

These speak eloquently of the refined approach to the appreciation of flowers, which could become evident only in an age of great aesthetic elegance.

Five centuries later, Yüan Hung-tao in his *P'ing Shih,* or History of Vases, expresses his admiration of Chang's discourse and, pat-

96

Plate 17.
BLUE AND WHITE VASES OF THE MING DYNASTY
Upper left: Kuan-type vase; *upper right:* Mei P'ing (Japanese Apricot vase)
or One-twig vase; *lower left:* Gourd-shaped vase; *lower right:* Paper-beater vase.

Plates 18-19. **FLOWER BASKETS OF THE FOUR SEASONS**
Woodblock prints by Ting Liang-hsien, 17th century. *Spring:* Magnolia, Peony,
Crab-apple. *Summer:* Pomegranate, Lotus, Day-lily. *Autumn:* Chrysanthemum
and Hibiscus. *Winter:* Wintersweet, Camellia, Narcissus.

Plate 20. INTERIOR DECORATIONS

Scene from the play "West Chamber," with the leading figures Chang and his
loved one; detail from a painting on silk by an unknown artist, 17th century.
Cymbidium and Rose in vase and Buddha's Hand Citron in bowl on table in
front. Dianthus in vase together with books and other decorations on book-and-
curio shelf. Ling-chih Fungus in a square vessel with books on rear table in
front of a hanging scroll of landscape painting. The moon window with curtains
separates the inner room, a studio from the porch.

terned after it, gives fourteen delightful conditions for enjoying flowers in general.

1. Bright window
2. Clear room
3. Ancient bronze tripods (incense burner)
4. Sung ink-stone
5. Wind among pines
6. Song of streams
7. The host loving hobbies and versed in poetry
8. Visiting monk understands brewing tea
9. Man of Chichow delivering wine
10. Guest skilled in painting flowers
11. An intimate friend arrives when flowers are in full bloom
12. Copying books on flower culture
13. Kettle sings deep in the night
14. Wife and concubines editing flower lores

Yüan was the most eloquent author on the subject of flower enjoyment. Excerpts from his writing in the *History of Vases* will be freely quoted here. On the love of flowers as a hobby, he writes:

"I have found people in the world who, unsavory in their conversation and detestable in their appearance, are those that are without hobbies. Those who have real hobbies often submerge themselves entirely with their very life and death, and have no time for affairs like money, slaves, official posts and business.

"In ancient times, persons really fond of flowers, when hearing of a strange flower, would not hesitate to search for it across deep gorges and precipitous peaks. They ignored bitter cold and torrid heat and were oblivious to peeling skin and dirty sweat. When a flower was about to bud, they would move their bedding to sleep under it, watching its change from the very beginning until its full bloom, and would leave only when it dropped to the ground.

"Sometimes thousands of plants were studied to seek their variations. Sometimes a single twig with several buds was examined to exhaust the interest. Sometimes one would be able to tell the size of the flowers from smelling the leaves, and sometimes one would be able to distinguish the color of the flowers from looking at the root. These were the true lovers of flowers, and this was what I called a true hobby."

Time and Place

On the proper time and place to enjoy flowers, Yüan gave the following illuminating account:

"Enjoying flowers with tea is the best, enjoying them with conversation the second, and enjoying them with wine the last. Feasts and all sorts of ordinary, vulgar language are most deeply detested and resented by the spirits of the flowers. It is better to keep the mouth shut and sit still than to offend the flowers.

"There is a proper place and a proper time to enjoy flowers. Inviting friends without considering the proper time is rudeness to the flowers. The time to enjoy winter flowers should be at the beginning and ending of snow, or during a new moon, or in a warm room. Spring flowers should be enjoyed under clear sun, or on a slightly chilly day, or in a beautiful hall. Summer flowers should be enjoyed after rain, in a refreshing breeze, in the shade of fine trees, under bamboos, or in a water pavilion. Autumn flowers should be enjoyed under a clear moon, at sunset, on empty steps, along a mossy path, or by the side of rugged rocks overhung with old vines.

"If one looks at flowers without considering wind or sun and without selecting the proper setting, or with one's thought wandering about without any relation to the flowers, what is the difference from seeing flowers in sing-song houses and wine saloons?"

In Peking, where Yüan wrote his book on flower arrangement, frequent storms carry dust to the city in large quantities. He thus found it necessary to spray, or "bathe" as he called it, vase flowers every day. Regarding this subject, his insight into the moods of the flowers shows his sentimental approach as only a real lover of flowers can envisage. He also calls attention to the different types of companions with which different flowers can be enjoyed. He writes thus:

"In the capital, wind storm is vagrant. Whenever it blows, on window sills and clean tables, dust thickly settles. The suffering

98

of vase flowers is utmost. Thus flowers should be bathed every day. . . . For flowers have moods of happiness and sadness, and wakefulness and sleep, and mornings and nights. Bathing flowers at the right time is like beneficial rains.

"Thin clouds and mild sun, and sunset and bright moonlight are mornings to flowers. Roaring winds and unceasing rains, and scorching sun and intense cold are evenings to the flowers. When their blossoms bask in the sun and their delicate bodies hide from the wind, the flowers are in a happy mood. When they appear drunk or tired, and the air is smoky and misty, the flowers are in a sad mood. When their branches incline and rest on the side as if they cannot stand the wind, the flowers are sleeping. When they seem to be smiling and glancing around, bright and gleaming, the flowers are awake.

"When the flowers are awake, place them in open courts or large halls. When they are asleep, place them in winding alleys or dark rooms. When they are sad, sit quiet and abate the breath. When they are happy, one can laugh and shout and play around. When they are asleep, let down the curtains and screens. When they are awake, one can attend to his daily toils. This is to please their nature and to keep in time with their living habits.

"To bathe the flowers when they are awake is the best; to bathe them when they are asleep is the next; while to bathe them when they are happy is the last. But the most undesirable is to bathe them while they are in the evening or in sorrow, which to flowers is like punishing them.

"The method of bathing is to use sweet and clear spring water and pour and spray in very little quantities, like a beneficial sprinkle which clears the drunken state and like a sparkling dew which soothes the body. One should not touch the flowers by hand or pick at them with finger tips. Also to be avoided is to let stupid servants attend to the affair. To bathe Mei (Japanese Apricot), it is best to have a recluse scholar. To bathe Crab-apples, it is best to have a charming guest. To bathe Peonies, it is best to have a fashionable young lady. To bathe Pomegranate, it is best to have a beautiful maid. To bathe Lotus, it is best to have a Taoist priest.

"Bathing"
of Flowers

To bathe Chrysanthemum, it is best to have one who prefers every-thing that is old and extraordinary. To bathe Wintersweet, it is best to have a slender monk. But flowers of the cold season do not stand bathing. They should be, instead, protected by thin silk gauze.

"When the characters of the flowers are appropriately developed, their spirit naturally radiates with brilliance. Not only do the flowers appear brighter and more lustrous, but their very life can thus be lengthened."

It is beyond doubt that only the utmost care given to the flowers will bring out their best. And it is only in their best conditions that one can fully enjoy their companionship, admire their beauty, and truly appreciate these wonderments of nature.

NINE HIGHEST PRIZES TO BE BESTOWED ON THE BEST FLOWERS

Double-topped curtain (for protecting from wind)
Gold scissors (for cutting)
Sweet spring water (for storing)
Jade vessels (for holding)
Carved stand (for resting)
Paintings
Ballads
Good wine (for enjoying)
New verses (to eulogize)

Lu Hung (Tang Dynasty)

100

Appendix I
A Treatise of Vase Flowers
by Chang Ch'ien-tê

Chang Ch'ien-tê was an author of the Ming dynasty living toward the end of the sixteenth century and the early seventeenth century. He was a native of Kunshan, a neighboring city of Soochow in Kiangsu province in eastern China. He wrote the most authoritative work on Chinese flower arrangement, *P'ing Hua Pu*, or *A Treatise of Vase Flowers*, in 1595, while he was still very young. The text is translated below.

PREFACE

Among the things of refined living, flower arrangement is the most difficult. Not one in a million can explain it. In former times, Chin Ren wrote a literary treatise when he was only a young boy. I am also in my boyhood writing these lines. Whether they are right or wrong, and to be followed or not, the understanding readers will make their fair criticism. It is not necessary for me to add more words here.

GRADING VASES

To make flower arrangement, it is necessary to select first the vessel. In spring and winter, the choice is bronze, while in summer and autumn, it is porcelain. This is in accordance with the seasons. In halls, the vessel should be large; in the study, small. This

101

is in accordance with the location. Porcelain and bronze wares are preferred, while gold and silver pieces are less valued. This is to show refinement. The vessels should not have rings on the side and they should not be in pairs, looking like temple decorations. They should have a small mouth and thick base, so they will be steady and will not lose vapors.

In general, it is better to have slender rather than stout vessels, and small rather than overly big ones. The tallest should not be over one foot in height. Vases of six and seven or four and five inches are best for flower arrangements. If the vessels are too small, they cannot nourish flowers for a long time.

Among the bronze shapes that can be used for flower arrangement are Ts'un, P'ing, Ku and Hu. These vessels were originally used for holding wine and now they are used for holding flowers. This seems to be very appropriate. (Figure 7.)

Ancient bronze wares, long buried underground, absorbed deeply the atmosphere of the earth. When they are used for holding flowers, the flowers have a fresh and bright appearance, as if they were intact on the original plant. They open more rapidly and wilt more slowly. Or when the flowers wilt, they will bear fruit while still in the vase. Only ancient wares using clear water behave like this. Potteries buried for a thousand years in the earth do the same.

In ancient times, there were no porcelain wares and all vessels were made of bronze. Not until the T'ang dynasty did ceramic wares become developed. Later, there were kiln wares of Ch'ai, Ju, Kuan, Ko, Ting, Lung-chüan, Chün-chou, Chang-shêng, Wu-ni, Hsüan, Ch'êng, etc., and the kinds became very numerous.

To cherish things ancient, bronze wares are of course the best. Among the ceramics, the most valuable ones are Ch'ai and Ju wares, but these are now scarcely preserved. The most precious wares at present are Kuan, Ko, Hsüan and Ting wares. And vases of Lung-chüan, Chün-chou, Chang-shêng, Wu-ni and Ch'êng-hua are also gradually becoming treasured. (Plate XII.)

Among the porcelain wares, the different kinds of ancient Hu, the gall vase, Ts'un, Ku and one-twig vase are most suitable for the study. Next to these, the little yarrow vase, paper-beater vase, round-plain vase and goose-necked wall vase can also be used for arranging flowers. The others, such as vases of hidden decoration, eggplant pouch, gourd-like, narrow-mouthed, flat-bellied, slender-legged medicine jars and vases are not suitable for elegant decorations. (Plates 17, XIV & Figures 9 & 10.)

Among the ancient bronze vessels and Lung-chüan and Chün-chou porcelain vessels, there are some of very large size with a height of over two or three feet. These have little use, but can be adapted for arranging large branches of Mei flowers (Japanese Apricot) in winter, with some sulphur in the water.

GRADING FLOWERS

One of the learned ancestors of our family prepared a table depicting the ascending and descending of flowers according to the nine official ranks. This is indeed an attempt to reduce the multitude of nature to the very point of the pen, and to depict a mystical image on a small piece of paper. Now that I am treating of vase flowers, it seems desirable also to grade the several tens of the more suitable ones for arrangement according to their relative merits into these nine classes.

Class I

Spring Cymbidium	*(Cymbidium virescens)*
Moutan Peony	*(Paeonia suffruticosa)*
Japanese Apricot	*(Prunus mume)*
Wintersweet	*(Chimonanthus praecox)*
Chrysanthemum	*(Chrysanthemum hortorum)*
Narcissus or Chinese Sacred **Lily**	*(Narcissus tazetta* var. *orientalis)*
Yunnan Camellia	*(Camellia reticulata)*
Spring Daphne	*(Daphne odora)*
Sweetflag	*(Acorus gramineus)*

Class II

Summer Cymbidium	*(Cymbidium ensifolium)*
Brier Rose	*(Rubus coronarius)*
Midget Crab-apple	*(Malus micromalus)*
Arabian Jasmine	*(Jasminum sambac)*

103

Camellia   *(Camellia japonica)*
Osmanthus   *(Osmanthus fragrans)*
Water Chestnut   *(Trapa natans)*
Pines   *(Pinus spp.)*
Banana Shrub   *(Michelia fuscata)*
Tea   *(Thea sinensis)*

Class III

Herbaceous Peony   *(Paeonia albiflora)*
Double-flowered Peach   *(Prunus persica)*
Lotus   *(Nelumbo nucifera)*
Early Lilac   *(Syringa oblata)*
Cuspidata Camellia   *(Camellia cuspidata)*
Bamboos   *(Phyllostachys spp.,* etc.)

Class IV

Asiatic Sweetleaf   *(Symplocos prunifolia)*
Silk Tree   *(Albizzia julibrissin)*
Chloranthus   *(Chloranthus spicatus)*
Multiflora Rose   *(Rosa multiflora)*
Chinese Begonia   *(Begonia evansiana)*
Mallow   *(Malva sylvestris)*
Apricot   *(Prunus armeniaca)*
Lily Magnolia   *(Magnolia liliflora)*
Double-flowered
  Pomegranate   *(Punica granatum)*
Chinese Hibiscus   *(Hibiscus rosa-sinensis)*
Pear   *(Pyrus serotina)*

Class V

Rugosa Rose   *(Rosa rugosa)*
Champac Michelia   *(Michelia champaca)*
Crape Myrtle   *(Lagerstroemia indica)*
Yellow Day Lily   *(Hemerocallis flava)*
Orange Day Lily   *(Hemerocallis fulva)*
Globosum Galangal   *(Alpinia globosum)*

Class VI

Yulan Magnolia   *(Magnolia denudata)*

104

Winter Jasmine	*(Jasminum nudiflorum)*
Cotton Rose	*(Hibiscus mutabilis)*
Common Jasmine	*(Jasminum officinale)*
Willow (young branches)	*(Salix spp.)*
Sasanqua Camellia	*(Camellia sasanqua)*

Class VII

Pea Tree	*(Caragana chamlagu)*
Chinese Azalea	*(Rhododendron molle)*
Chinese Matrimony Vine	*(Lycium chinense)*
Caesalpinia	*(Caesalpinia pulcherrima)*
Double-flowered	
Japanese Plum	*(Prunus salicina)*
Trifoliate Orange	*(Poncirus trifoliata)*
Indian Azalea	*(Rhododendron simsii)*

Class VIII

Double-flowered	
Hollyhock	*(Althaea rosea)*
Plantain Lily	*(Hosta glauca)*
Cock's Comb	*(Celosia argenta)*
Chinese Pink	*(Dianthus chinensis)*
Chinese Crab-apple	*(Malus prunifolia)*
Okra	*(Hibiscus esculentus)*

Class IX

Chinese Campion	*(Lychnis coronaria)*
Galangal	*(Alpinia officinarum)*
Stone Crop	*(Sedum japonicum)*
Asiatic Morning Glory	*(Convolvulus japonicus)*
"Bamboo-leaved Grass"	*(Lophatherum elatum)*

PICKING BRANCHES

To cut flowers, it is best to go to the nearest garden, and in the early morning before the dew disappears. Choose half-opened ones for arrangement, and their color and fragrance will not diminish for several days. Flowers cut later in the day, after the dew has dried, not only do not have sufficient fragrance and brightness in color, but will also wilt in only one or two days.

In picking flowers, it is necessary to select first the branch. The stem may be luxuriant above and slender below. It may be taller on the left and shorter on the right, or vice versa. It may have two branches crisscrossing each other, gnarled and crooked in shape. It may have a stout vigorous stalk in the center, sparse atop and be dense below, covering the mouth of the vase. Whether ascending or hanging, tall or low, sparse or dense, and oblique or upright, the branches that have natural beauty must show the appealing features of cut flowers as depicted by the painter. Straight branches and windblown flowers are not suitable for refined arrangement.

Both herbaceous and woody stems can be used for arranging in vases. There are two ways of cutting them: use fingers for herbaceous plants and scissors for woody ones. One who considers himself a lover of flowers should take note of this.

It is easy to select and cut woody stems for their best features, while it is most difficult to select and cut herbaceous ones. It is hard to achieve exquisiteness except by intensive study of masterpieces of flower painting.

ARRANGING

Cut flowers and branches must be immediately put into a small-mouthed vase. Tightly seal the opening to avoid losing vapors, and the flowers can be enjoyed for several days.

In general, arranged flowers should be in proportion to the size of the vase. It is best to have the branches of slightly longer length than the vase. If the vase is one foot high, the flowers should be one foot three to four inches tall above the mouth of the vase. If the vase is six to seven inches tall, the flowers should be eight to nine inches above the mouth of the vase. Flowers should not be too tall, as the vase will easily tilt. They should not be too low to upset the beauty of the composition.

When using a small vase for arranging flowers, the branches should be slender and exquisite, not dense and mussy. If a single branch is used, select one that is of curious and aged appearance, one which is gnarled and crooked. When two different kinds of flowers are used, they should be of different height and, when

106

placed together, look as if they were grown naturally from a single stalk. If two branches are grown in opposite directions, rearrange and fit them together as if they were originally grown like that, then tie them together with a hemp cord and put them in the vase.

Although tousle and muss should be avoided in flower arrangement, an even more undesirable situation is having the branches thinner than the vase. It is necessary to cut oblique and slanting branches and spread them on both sides of the small vase to achieve the proper balance.

Only one or two kinds of flowers should be arranged in a vase. If too many different kinds are used together, they are unappealing. The only exceptions are autumn flowers.

WATERING

Flowers live by the nourishment of rain and dew. To use rain water in a vase is to let the flowers have the benefit of rain and dew. Some flowers need honey in the water while others need boiling water. It is up to the connoisseurs of flowers to devise ways according to the material.

It is often necessary to store quantities of rain water to have on hand for use as the first choice for nourishing flowers. If this cannot be had, use clear and clean water from lakes and rivers. Do not use water from wells, as it is often salty and, if used, the flowers will not grow well.

When water is used for flowers in a vase, it gradually accumulates harmful matters. Change the water every day and the flowers will keep fresh for a longer period. If it is not changed for two or three days, the flowers will often fade or drop.

Vase flowers should be placed in a sheltered place outside the room at night for exposure to the dew. This will prolong the life of the flowers for several days.

METHODS OF PREPARATION

For Mei Hua (Japanese Apricot), as soon as picked, it is recommended to singe the cut end of the branch and seal it with dirt. For Moutan Peony, the twig should be heated over a flame at the end as soon as it is cut, until it becomes soft. For Champac Michelia, the base of the picked stem should be first crushed and then rubbed with a little salt. For Lotus, it is recommended that the base of the flower stalk be wrapped with human hairs and then sealed with dirt. For Crab-apple, when first picked, the base of the stem should be wrapped with tender leaves of mint before being inserted in water.

For Peonies, the addition of a little honey in the water will prolong their freshness in the vase. For Bamboo, Hollyhock, Caesalpinia and Hibiscus, if boiling water is used, their leaves will not wilt easily.

INJURIES TO FLOWERS

Generally speaking, there are six things disadvantageous to vase flowers. The first is water from wells; second, not changing water frequently; third, handling the flowers with oily fingers; fourth, damage of the flowers by cats and rats; fifth, exposure to incense and smoke; and last, placing the flowers in closed and sealed rooms without letting them have the benefit of breeze and dew. Any one of these is detrimental to vase flowers.

PROTECTING THE VASE

In winter there are few desirable flowers except Narcissus, Wintersweet and Mei Hua (Japanese Apricot). During this season, it is best to use wide-mouthed ancient vases. When these are used for arranging flowers, use tin inner tubes for the water to avoid cracking the vase. If a small porcelain vase is used, it is necessary to add a little sulphur. If the vase is placed near the southern window in the sunshine in the day, and near the bed close to human warmth in the night, it will also not freeze. Another method is to use diluted meat broth, with fat completely removed, for use as water in the vase. The flowers will thrive and open as usual, while the vase will not be damaged by freezing.

In using boiling water, it is important to use first an ordinary jar or bottle for the water. Then place the twig in the bottle and seal the mouth tightly. When the water is cold, the twig can then be transferred to the chosen vase filled with rain water, so that the vase will not be damaged. Do not use boiling water directly in a valuable vase, as it will surely damage a precious piece.

108

Appendix II

A List of Common Chinese Flowers

The following list is limited to flowers of the classical Chinese garden, flowers indigenous to the country and long domesticated since early times, as well as a few exotics brought to China around the middle ages and since integrated into the Chinese garden flora. The very numerous flowers introduced into our gardens by modern explorers from the mountains of western China are not included.

Abelia chinensis	Abelia
Albizzia julibrissin	Silk Tree
Alpinia globosum	Globosum Galangal
A. officinarum	Galangal
Althaea rosea	Hollyhock
Anemone japonica	Japanese Anemony
Begonia evansiana	Chinese Begonia
Belamcanda chinensis	Blackberry Lily
Bletilla striata	"Purple Orchid"
Buddleja lindleyana	Butterfly Bush
Caesalpinia pulcherrima	Caesalpinia
Callistephus chinensis	Chinese Aster
Camellia cuspidata	Cuspidata Camellia
C. japonica	Camellia
C. reticulata	Yunnan Camellia
C. sasanqua	Sasanqua Camellia
Campsis grandiflora	Chinese Trumpet Creeper

109

Caragana chamlagu	Pea Tree
Chaenomeles lagenaria	Japanese Quince
Ch. sinensis	Chinese Flowering Quince
Chimonanthus praecox	Wintersweet
Chionanthus retusus	Chinese Fringed Tree
Chloranthus spicatus	Chloranthus
Chrysanthemum hortorum	Garden Chrysanthemum
Clematis florida	Clematis
Convolvulus japonicus	Asiatic Morning Glory
Cornus kousa chinensis	Chinese Dogwood
Cymbidium ensifolium	Summer Cymbidium
C. primulum	Primulum Cymbidium
C. virescens	Spring Cymbidium
Daphne genkwa	Lilac Daphne
D. odora	Spring Daphne
Delphinium grandiflorum	Larkspur
Deutzia scabra	Deutzia
Dianthus barbatus	Sweet William
D. chinensis	Chinese Pink
Dicentra spectabilis	Bleeding Heart
Forsythia suspensa	Golden Bell
F. viridissima	Golden Bell
Gardenia jasminoides	Gardenia or Cape Jasmine
Hamamelis mollis	Chinese Witch Hazel
Hemerocallis flava	Yellow Day Lily
H. fulva	Orange Day Lily
H. minor	Dwarf Day Lily
Hibiscus esculentus	Okra
H. manihot	Sunset Hibiscus
H. mutabilis	Cotton Rose
H. rosa-sinensis	Chinese Hibiscus
H. syriacus	Shrubby Althea
Hosta glauca	Plantain Lily
Hydrangea macrophylla hortensia	Hydrangea
Hypericum chinense	St. John's Wort

110

Impatiens balsamina	Garden Balsam
Iris ensata chinensis	Chinese Iris
I. japonica	Fringed Iris
I. laevigata	Japanese Iris
Jasminum nudiflorum	Winter Jasmine
J. officinale	Common Jasmine
J. sambac	Arabian Jasmine
Kerria japonica	Kerria
Lagerstroemia indica	Crape Myrtle
Lilium brownii	Musk Lily
L. concolor	Star Lily
L. tigrinum	Tiger Lily
Litsea glauca	Litsea
Lonicera japonica	Honeysuckle
Lychnis coronaria	Chinese Campion
Lycoris aurea	Yellow Lycoris
L. radiata	Red Lycoris
Magnolia denudata	Yulan Magnolia
M. liliflora ..	Lily Magnolia
Malus baccata	Siberian Crab-apple
M. floribunda	Showy Crab-apple
M. halliana	Hall Crab-apple
M. micromalus	Midget Crab-apple
M. prunifolia	Chinese Crab-apple
M. spectabilis	Crab-apple
Malva sylvestris	Mallow
Mangelietia fordiana	Mangelietia
Michelia champac	Champac Michelia
M. fuscata	Banana Shrub
Narcissus tazetta orientalis	Narcissus
Nelumbo nucifera	Lotus
Nerium indicum	Oleander
Osmanthus fragrans	Osmanthus
Paeonia albiflora	Herbaceous Peony

111

P.	*suffruticosa*	Moutan Peony
Papaver rhoeas		Corn Poppy
Paulownia tomentosa		Paulownia
Philadelphus pekinensis		Peking Mock Orange
Prunus armeniaca		Apricot
P.	*japonica*	Dwarf Flowering Cherry
P.	*mume*	Japanese Apricot
P.	*persica*	Peach
P.	*salicina*	Japanese Plum
P.	*triloba*	Flowering Almond
Punica granatum		Pomegranate
Pyrus serotina		Sand Pear
Quamoclit pennata		Cypress Vine
Rhododendron molle		Chinese Azalea
Rh.	*mucronatum*	Snow Azalea
Rh.	*pulchrum*	Lovely Azalea
Rh.	*simsii*	Indian Azalea
Rosa banksiae		Banksia Rose
R.	*chinensis*	Chinese Rose
R.	*laevigata*	Cherokee Rose
R.	*multiflora*	Multiflora Rose
R.	*rugosa*	Rugosa Rose
R.	*rubus*	Blackberry Rose
R.	*xanthina*	Yellow Prickly Rose
Rubus coronarius		Brier Rose
Sedum japonicum		Stone Crop
Spiraea blumei		Blume Spirea
Sp.	*cantoniensis*	Canton Spirea
Sp.	*prunifolia*	Bridal Wreath
Sp.	*thunbergii*	Thunberg Spirea
Stachyurus chinensis		Chinese Stachyurus
Syringa meyeri		Meyer Lilac
S.	*microphylla*	Small-leaved Lilac
S.	*oblata*	Early Lilac
S.	*pekinensis*	Peking Lilac

112

S.	*pubescens*	Hardy Lilac
S.	*villosa*	Late Lilac

Viburnum fragrans	Fragrant Vibrunum
V. *macrocephalum*	Chinese Snowball
V. *tomentosum*	Japanese Snowball

Weigela floribunda	Weigela
W. *florida*	Weigela
Wisteria sinensis	Chinese Wisteria

Appendix III

Chinese Dynasties

HSIA .... 2205-1766 B.C.

SHANG .... 1766-1122 B.C.

CHOU .... 1122- 249 B.C.
        Period of the "Spring and Autumn Annals"
                           722-481 B.C.
        Warring States .... 481-221 B.C.

CH'IN .... 221-206 B.C.

HAN .... 206 B.C.-220 A.D.
        Western Han .... 206 B.C.-25 A.D.
        Eastern Han .... 25-220 A.D.

WEI .... 220-265 A.D.
        Shu Han .... 221-263 A.D.
        Tung Wu .... 222-280 A.D.

TSIN .... 265-420 A.D.

NORTHERN and SOUTHERN DYNASTIES .... 386-589 A.D.
        Northern Dynasties .... 386-557 A.D.
        Northern Wei .... 386-557 A.D.
        Eastern Wei .... 534-550 A.D.
        Northern Ch'i .... 550-577 A.D.
        Northern Chou .... 557-581 A.D.
        Southern Dynasties .... 420-589 A.D.
        Sung (Liu) .... 420-479 A.D.
        Southern Ch'i .... 470-502 A.D.

Liang	502-557 A.D.
Ch'en	557-589 A.D.
SUI	589-618 A.D.
T'ANG	618-906 A.D.
FIVE DYNASTIES	907-960 A.D.
Liang	907-923 A.D.
T'ang	923-936 A.D.
Tsin	936-946 A.D.
Han	947-950 A.D.
Chou	951-960 A.D.
Liao	937-1125 A.D.
SUNG	960-1279 A.D.
Northern Sung	960-1127 A.D.
Southern Sung	1127-1279 A.D.
Chin	1115-1234 A.D.
Western Hsia	1032-1223 A.D.
YÜAN	1280-1368 A.D.
MING	1368-1644 A.D.
CH'ING	1644-1911 A.D.
REPUBLIC	1912- A.D.

Bibliography

Works in Chinese

Ch'ang Wu Chih (Record of Excellent Things), by Wen Chêng-hêng, early 17th century.

Chieh Tzŭ Yüan Hua Ch'uan (Painting Patterns of the Mustard Seed Garden), by Wang Kai, 1682 and 1701.

Fu Shêng Liu Chi (Six Chapters of a Floating Life), by Shen Fu, 19th century.

Hsien Ching Ou Chi (The Art of Living), by Li Chih, mid 17th century.

K'ao P'an Yü Shih (The Art of Refined Living), by T'u Lung, late 16th century.

Pi Ch'uan Hua Ching (Mirror of Flowers), by Ch'ên Hao-tzŭ, 1688.

P'ing Hua Pu (A Treatise of Vase Flowers), by Chang Ch'ien-tê, 1595.

P'ing Shih (History of Vases), by Yüan Hung-tao, end of 16th century.

P'ing Shih Yüeh Piao (Monthly Calender of Vase Flowers), by T'u Pêng-tsün, early 17th century.

Tsun Shêng Pa Chien (Eight Discourses on the Art of Living), by Kao Lien-shêng, 1591.

Works in English

Laufer, H. Chinese Baskets. Field Museum of Natural History Anthropology Design Ser. No. 3. 1925.

Li, H. L. The Garden Flowers of China. Ronald Press, N. Y. 1959.

Lin, Yutang. The Importance of Living. John Day, N. Y. 1937.

McClure, F. A. Methods and materials of Chinese table plant culture. In Lingnan Science Journal Vol. 12, Suppl. pp. 119-149. 1933.

Index

120

INDEX